For further information, please contact:
E-mail: leon@ethicallymad.com
Web: www.ethicallymad.com/superheroes
To learn more about the author, visit: www.leonjay.info.

CONTENTS

Foreword VII

Preface IX

Introduction 1

Part 1: Psychological Preparation   3

The Revolution Has Begun 5

How Serious Is Our Environmental Debt? 13

The Birth of the Real-Life Superhero 19

Real-Life Superhero Profile...23

The Hero's Journey...25

The Demon of Denial..31

The Demon of Self-Justification.......................................33

The Demon of Blame...37

Real-Life Superhero Profile...39

Choosing Your Path 43

The Emblem of Socialpreneurship 49

Real-Life Superhero Profile...53

Joining Forces 55

Two More Demons to Face 57

Meet Your Archenemy..61

Real-Life Superhero Profile...65

The Enemy Hiding in Plain Sight.......................................67

The Great Lie That May Destroy the World...........................71

Learning to Think Like a Superhero 77

Part 2:Strategies for War   81

Rules of the Game...83

Real-Life Superhero Profile...87

A Conflict of Interest 89

Close the Loop 93
An Efficient System 95
The Big 3 99
Air 101
Water 105
Food 109
The Singularity 113
Real-Life Superhero Profile 115
You Have the Power, Now Use It 117

Part 3: One-to-One Combat   121
The Primary Battlegrounds 123
Electricity 125
Transport 131
Plastic 139
Animal Agriculture 145
Clothing 155
Raw Materials 159
Real-Life Superhero Profile 165
Balancing the Forces of Good and Evil 167
Which Brings Us to Zenbags 175

Part 4: Grow Your Strength   179
Wherever There Is a Problem 181
Real-Life Superhero Profile 183
Marketing Madness 185
I Object! 189
The Keys to Happiness (and the Real-Life Superhero's True
Strength) 199
A Summary of Your Superpowers 201
Real-Life Superhero Profile 207

Part 5: Into the Future 211

Finding Help and Support 213

A Prediction of The Future 215

Epilogue 219

Join the Real-Life Superheroes Club (Free) 223

About the Author 225

Footnotes 227

FOREWORD

Capitalism is often blamed by many as the cause of our current world crisis. While there is a strong case for this argument, it is inherently flawed.

Capitalism can be defined as "an economic and political system in which a country's trade and industry are controlled by private owners for profit, rather than by the state."[1] This system has led to as much innovation and economic growth as it has greed and corruption.

It is not the system per se, but the abuse of the system that is the real issue. It is similar to the way some individuals have used the guise of religion to gain power and control. It is not religion's fault. It is simply how some people have chosen to interpret or take advantage of religion for personal gain.

Let me be very clear: profit is not the enemy of environmentalism. Nor is capitalism. Indeed, there are many companies that make good profits while working to make the world a better place.

Throughout this book, Leon guides you along the hero's path and helps you make the transformation from just another business trying to make a buck, to a well-paid superhero that is doing their part to save the world.

Prepare for a rollercoaster of a ride!

PREFACE

This book is meant as a guide for entrepreneurs and business owners who want to help make the world a better place, and who want to make their businesses more meaningful.

Throughout this book, a lot of environmental statistics are used to help illustrate the need for action, highlight areas for improvement, and opportunities for businesses to create solutions to the current challenges. The truth is though, the exact numbers are rarely known, and there is a wide range of expert opinions that don't always agree on the specifics. However, this is not reason to dismiss the underlying message.

Many sceptics will try question any piece of research, often believing if they can find error in the data then the problem does not exist. This only leads to intellectual arrogance and procrastination. You don't need to be a genius to know we have problems. The details and severity of the current situation can be debated all day long, but does little to change the simple need for businesses to urgently become more socially and environmentally responsible.

With that said, I urge you to set aside your internal critic, and read this book with an open mind in its entirety before passing judgment.

*This book is dedicated to all those who are caring through
action, putting planet and people first, and have earned
Their place amongst the legions of Real-Life Superheroes*

*Not one individual can save the world.
But every individual can save a bit of it,
And together we can save all of it.*

"UNLESS SOMEONE LIKE YOU CARES A WHOLE AWFUL LOT, NOTHING IS GOING TO GET BETTER. IT'S NOT." - THE LORAX

INTRODUCTION

> "Nobody can go back and start a new beginning, but anyone can start today and make a new ending."
> —Maria Robinson

It was a dark and stormy night. The rain was coming down hard, and the only light came from the frequent but short flashes of lightning that appeared to tear the very fabric of the universe.

It was during one of these flashes that I caught the movement of a silhouette lurking between the trees. Was it man or beast? There was no way to know. I could feel a chill go down my spine as I began to realize the full extent of the danger I had unwittingly put myself in. But I had no choice. The laws of the space-time continuum dictated that I must keep moving forward. I was about to face my darkest fears...

Well, okay, a little melodramatic. But if this book were a very dark action-comedy movie, chances are it would have started something like that.

The adventure we are about to embark on together will require you to face truths you have been trying to hide from. It will force you to face your fears. It will be a journey that will, at times, border on Gothic in its morbid perspective. But, my brave warrior, don't give up.

Like any good story, we will find the light. Good can prevail. And, as every hero who finds the courage to face his fears will discover, when faced head-on, many fears prove little more than an illusion of the mind.

However, along the way we will see there are many shadows hiding in the dark that should concern us. Once identified, they will become increasingly difficult to ignore, but you will also see there are ways to defeat these demons. We will also find time for a few comic moments to help lift our spirits, and we will see there is plenty that offers hope for our future. You will discover this is more like a choose-your-own-adventure with many possible endings, rather than a finished movie script.

The book is broken into five stages. The first part is a look into the motivation and path of the superhero. The second and third parts provide the mental and emotional training required, along with important strategic approaches. The fourth section will get into specifics of what you can do today that reduces your environmental impact while reducing costs and increasing revenue. The final section takes a quick look at where to next.

As your guide on this journey, I will at times be encouraging and supportive. Other times I will need to be blunt and direct. Please don't take this personally. The truth can at times hurt, but this pain is unfortunately necessary, and thankfully only temporary.

The good news is,you will discover you are not powerless. You can change the ending. You don't need to be the victim or the villain in this epic saga. You can be the hero.

PART 1: PSYCHOLOGICAL PREPARATION

> "If something is important enough, you should try, even if the probable outcome is failure."
>
> —Elon Musk

THE REVOLUTION HAS BEGUN

> "You're going to make a difference. A lot of times
> it won't be huge, it won't be visible even.
> But it will matter just the same."
>
> **—Commissioner James Gordon**

We are in the middle of a planetary civil war. It is a war with more casualties and consequences than any previously fought here on earth. And it is a war that every single man, woman, and child is fighting, even if they have yet to realize it.

It is a fight against ourselves for our very own survival. And right now, we are losing.

This is not a book about climate change(though that may well be a significant part of the problem). This is a book about how we are destroying the very balance of the world we live in at almost every level And, more importantly, what we can do about it.

Global warming gets more than its fair share of media attention. But this is just the tip of the (very rapidly melting) iceberg Industry is also responsible for polluting the land, the water, and the air,which are all essential for our survival.

This impact of industry on our environment has wiped out thousands of species in an incredibly short period of time, with literally dozens more being lost every single day. It has been responsible, directly and indirectly, for the deaths of untold human lives. And it has caused sickness and suffering for many hundreds of millions (billions?) more.

There is a harsh truth that we don't want to face: we have built up a massive environmental debt. And, if this debt is not paid soon, we will go environmentally bankrupt. We have taken far more from nature than we have ever given back. Until recently, our debts have been mounting with little more than a letter of warning. Unfortunately, as with any loan, there is only so long we can keep increasing the debt without repercussions—and those repercussions are exactly what we face now.

I am not pointing the finger at any one person. If only it were that simple. Indeed,almost every single individual on this planet has contributed. While many may be ignorant as to their part in this conflict, not one person reading this book is innocent. *Ignorantia legis neminem excusat* "ignorance of the law excuses no one." And right now, we are breaking the laws of sustainability and ecological balance.

Here is another harsh reality we must face: nature does not care if we survive or not. We only need look at how it has repeatedly wiped out species, and countless humans, through five mass extinctions and endless natural disasters. With forest fires, volcanoes,tsunamis, floods, tornadoes, droughts, plagues, and a multitude of other methods, nature has killed and injured millions of humans, along with incalculable plants and animals.

If we want to survive, it is up to us. It does not look like any gods or aliens are coming to save us anytime soon. (Though I am open to being wrong on this, I don't think it is something we should be relying on!)

It would appear that the human race would prefer to eat, drive,text, and buy its way to sickness and death(while taking down millions of other helpless species with it), rather than give up its destructive behaviors. That includes me, you, and probably everyone else we know.

Don't believe me?

We all make choices every day. What we wear, which companies we work for(or work with), what transport we use, what products we buy, what food we eat, and which services we use. And despite the marketing, not one of them is truly "green." Not the local organic store, hemp clothing chain, eco-friendly laundry powder, solar panel kit, or the electric car you may choose. With perhaps some very rare exceptions, they can't be.

Every business relies on the products and services of other businesses. And this web of businesses is filled with a story of pollution, consumption of limited resources, and social injustice.

Terms such as natural, organic, eco, and green may make us feel better about the products we buy,but be under no illusion, not one of them is 100 percent environmentally friendly. At this point in history, the best they can hope to be is a shade greener than the competition.

This civil war is one that even the good guys can't help but to assist the enemy. At least not for now.

As Aldous Huxley pointed out, "Facts do not cease to exist because they are ignored."[2] Sticking our head in the sand and trying to ignore what is happening won't make the consequences any less devastating.

Your only hope of being completely neutral is to strip naked, live in a cave, sleep under leaves, and eat wild berries (ideally not the poisonous ones). However, unless the majority of the planet did this, the only likely outcome from this effort would be a degrading nickname (like "Wild Willy of the Woods") and probable arrest for indecent exposure. No, if you want to change the results of the game, you must first be in the game.

But there is hope. There is something we can do.

In every war there are certain individuals who will influence the final outcome more than most. And if you are an entrepreneur or business owner, then you are one of these key people who have that power—even if you try to deny it.

Let me explain . . .

Usually social and environmental blame is broken into three key camps: consumers, politicians, and businesses.

Consumers (and we are all consumers) can only choose from the solutions offered to them by businesses. Almost every customer when provided the proper education will make the "right" choice—so long as it is financially equivalent (or at least economically viable) and not a compromise in quality.

Depending on the individual, and level of social pressure, the range of compromise on quality or cost can be pushed a little. But you will always, especially for those with lower education or incomes, get a significant percentage who will make price the deciding factor above all else.

Consumers do have an influence through their buying choices, but their choice and influence remain limited to what is available.

Many politicians mean well, while others are just corrupt or misinformed as to the real problems. Either way, they are part of a system that is driven by public demand, and by pressure from big business.

Time and time again we have seen insufficient or ineffective laws being passed to address the current environmental crisis. Unfortunately, politics is often too slow and funded (guided) by the objectives of large corporations.

Politicians do have some power, of course, and some make a significant contribution to humanity's rescue mission. By helping pass stronger laws for protecting the world's resources, forcing industry to reduce waste and pollution, and protecting workers' rights,the political system does make a difference. But that difference is also limited and, on its own, inadequate.

At the preview of Leonardo DiCaprio's documentary Before the Flood(which was held on the White House lawn), in his final days as president, Barak Obama expressed his concerns about climate change. This is a man that held the most politically powerful position in the world for eight years,during one of the most environmentally critical periods of human history. Yet despite his beliefs on climate change, he was unable to create sufficient policy change to address the problem adequately.

If you have been relying on politics to save the world, then think again. If we wait for the political system, it is almost certainly going to be too late. And ultimately,politicians don't create the end products that consumers rely on. No, that's up to business.

It is business activity that got us into this mess. Period.

It is business that cleared forests to raise animals or grow mono crops. It is business that produces the chemicals that pollute our world. It is business that builds the cars which pump out CO_2. And it is business that generates most of the energy we consume, and every product or service we purchase.

Many people blame consumer demand for driving business behavior, but no one is forcing businesses to do what they do the way that they do it. It is also the marketing techniques employed by businesses that generate the desire in consumers to buy far more than they need (or can afford). And this excess consumption only amplifies the overall negative impact.

Consumers may try to turn a blind eye to what happens behind the scenes, but ignorance is only bliss right up unto the point you get burnt. Ultimately though, it is the business owners' responsibility to ensure that they are doing the right thing, and the consumers' responsibility to support the right businesses.

Yup, it is doing business that got us into this mess,and it is up to business to get us out. As entrepreneurs and business owners, we are the biggest points of leverage in turning the tide on this war against our planet.

Why wait for politicians to change laws to tell us what we can or cannot do if we already know what needs to be done? We can make better decisions today, choose to focus our resources on creating increasingly green solutions, and use our marketing budgets to educate consumers to make better buying decisions.

I consider myself a realist. This will only happen if we can maintain a sufficient degree of profit. And,to ensure economic, environmental, and social sustainability, that is exactly what must happen. Making profit is not the enemy. Greed, ignorance, and stupidity are.

Throughout this book, we will look at how you can become a Real-Life Superhero by helping make the world a better place, and at the same time maintain or increase your profits.

Yes, every one of us is in the midst of a fight for personal survival and for the survival of future generations. We may try to ignore the civil war raging around us, but in doing so we make ourselves our own worst enemy.

At the end of the day, it is your actions not your words that define which side you are really fighting for. Personally, I believe this war to be a critical challenge, and we should do our utmost to find peace. Even if the probable outcome is failure. I hope you do too.

Numbers of many **large marine** life species have **reduced to 90%** of their original size.[4]

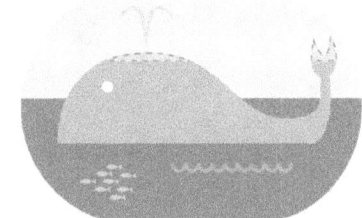

5.5 million people die each year from **air pollution**[3]

12.6 million people are dying every year due to environmental pollution[5]

1 in 5 species currently face **extinction**. This number is set to increase to 1 in 2 by the end of the century.[6]

We have an approximately **1 in 8** chance of all being **wiped out** by the end of the century.

That means you now have a greater chance to die in **Amrageddon** than a **car crash**.[7]

One child dies every **10 seconds** from some malnutrition related cause.[8]

HOW SERIOUS IS OUR ENVIRONMENTAL DEBT?

> "We'll lose more species of plants and animals between 2000 and 2065 than we've lost in the last 65 million years. If we don't find answers to these problems, we're gonna be victims of this extinction event that we're at fault for."
> —Paul Franklin Watson

If Paul is correct (and there is plenty of science to suggest that he is), then the situation is serious indeed. This level of severity is almost impossible to comprehend. As Professor Albert A. Bartlett observed, "The greatest shortcoming of the human race is our inability to understand the exponential function."[9] Yet this is exactly what we are up against.

Since the '70s there have been warnings of climate change, and a cry for environmental action. But we have continued business as usual. With a few exceptions, such as banning CFCs and whaling, we have done disturbingly little to prevent any of the anticipated disasters. (Yes, I know we have increased the amount of solar power production, started producing biodegradable plastics, etc., but most of this has been in addition to, not a replacement for, existing bad business practices.)

And yet the world has not come to an end. Many would argue that the economy, though a little bumpy, is as good as ever, and humans are living at a higher standard than ever before. So why all the fuss?

Consider these words:

Climate change at a rate faster than at any time since the end of the ice age—change too fast perhaps for life to adapt, without severe dislocation . . .Tropical islands barely afloat even now, first made inhabitable, and then obliterated beneath the waves . . . coastal lowlands everywhere suffering pollution of precious groundwater, on which so much farming and so many cities

> *depend . . . Our numbers are many, and infinitely diverse. But the problems and dilemmas of climatic change concern us all.*[10]

And the source for this enlightened insight? Climate of Concern, a film produced by Shell back in 1991. Yes, the very same company that has spent the twenty-five years since pumping oil, investing in highly polluting tar sands extraction, and lobbying against actions that could prevent climate change.

The reality is, we are all in for a serious wake-up call. In much the same way that many companies and investors had a rude awakening during the dot-com bust of 2000, and again during the 2008 financial crisis, we are about to wake up from the delusional bubble we have created for ourselves. Only this time we are facing a much, much bigger problem.

The consequences of our actions are just beginning, and no matter what we do now, they are about to get a whole lot worse. If we act now, we may well just steer ourselves back from the brink of extinction. If not, we are likely to gain too much momentum, and no amount of effort will stop the inevitable train wreck.

Regardless of what may happen in the future, we don't need scientists or computer modeling to know that we have serious problems today. Here is just a tiny snapshot of why EVERY business owner needs to stop thinking only about their back pocket, and start thinking about the world they are leaving for their children, as well as the billions of other lives they are indirectly affecting.

- UNICEF reported 22,000 children die every day due to poverty.[11]

- The world's wealthiest 20 percent consume 76.6 percent of all the world's resources (and produce an equivalent percentage of waste and environmental damage).[12]

- The world's wealthiest 10 percent are responsible for 49 percent of the world's waste.[13] That's over three times as much damage as even the next top 10 percent.

- If everyone on the planet consumed the same way as the average American, we would need another 4.1 planetearths to provide the food and resources required.[14] As populations and economies continue to rise, so too do the inadequacies of our planet.

- Trees remain one of our best defenses again increasing CO_2 levels, yet we keep cutting down three to six billion of them every year.[15] Much of this loss is so we can produce more meat.

- We are literally in the process of creating the sixth planetary mass extinction (yet few people are talking about it). Species are currently becoming extinct at a rate of between 1,000 times and 10,000 times the usual natural rate. That is dozens every day (instead of the previous 1–5 per year).[16] And human activity is the cause of almost all of them.

- 5.5 million people die every year as a result of air pollution.[17] Many of these deaths are in China and India, where we outsource our dirty work. We may choose not to look, but we are a part of their cause.

- Estimates by David Pimentel from Cornell University suggest that 40 percent of all human death is caused by pollution.[18] This includes air, water, and soil.

- Currently natural disasters displace more people than war, and this trend is on the rise.[19] We are now experiencing more extreme floods, droughts, and storms than ever before in recorded history, and this increase is expected to continue. We will likely see an exponential rather than incremental growth in this pattern, with weather spiraling out of control in the next few decades.

- Streets in Miami are already flooding, even on a sunny day, due to sea level rises.[20] Other cities and nations are also experiencing the early effects of the rapidly warming waters.[21]

- In just one week of February 2017, 736 record highs were recorded across the US, with many places experiencing summer temperatures.[22]

- According to a report by the WWF, we have lost 20 percent of our remaining mangroves in the last twenty-five years alone, tuna and mackerel populations have declined by 74 percent in forty years, and currently 1 in 4 species of sharks and rays are facing extinction (primarily due to industrial pollution and overfishing).[23]

- As atmospheric CO_2 levels rise, oceans absorb more of the gas to become increasingly acidic (forming a weak carbonic acid).Levels are already so bad that many oysters and other shellfish cannot survive, as their shells are being eroded away by the acidic environment.

- The US alone produces 220 million tons of waste every year. Much of this is decomposing to produce methane, adding to the 90 million tons of methane generated by livestock farming every year.[24]

And this is just a tiny snapshot.

In addition to all this damage, we have also experienced a tenfold increase in clinical depression since 1945[25] , along with soaring cancer[26], heart disease[27], and diabetes rates.[28]

If you are one of those people finding fault with this data, then you are missing the point. It is always easy to pick holes in research that has conducted on a global scale. The reality is we are in an undeniable mess, and being cynical or nit picking over specific numbers does little more than create apathy.

Of course, it is not all bad, but it would be foolish to remain in denial of the negative impact that our choices have caused,and continue to cause.

The real problem is that when a woman in Beijing dies from air pollution, it is impossible to point the finger at one individual for causing her death. Yet these types of death are directly attributable to the impact of many businesses which continue to trade without considering the effects they are having.

One company may look at its pollution output and say that it is low and not enough to harm anyone. But when you combine millions of businesses with the same attitude, you have a serious problem.

There is hope. Unfortunately, it relies on every business owner putting his or her greed aside, starting to take responsibility, and working together to find solutions.

Driving an electric vehicle does not mean you are doing your bit for the world. It is a step in the right direction, but we need to be brutally honest with ourselves: this is just an insufficient drop in the bucket, and on its own will do little to resolve the list of problems mentioned so far.

We face some thought-provoking challenges ahead. The (very elusive) Joshua J. Marine may offer some inspiration in this regard with his wise words: "Challenges are what make life interesting; overcoming them is what makes life meaningful."Never before has there been opportunity for a more meaningful life as an entrepreneur.

We are using **96.4 million** barrels of oil per day.[29]

We cut down **fifty million** acres of forest every year.[30]

We pollute our environment with **5.2 billion** pounds of pesticides every year. (Only 10 percent have been tested for safety, and many of these remain controversial.)[31]

0.5%

We use **one million** plastic bags per minute (with only around 0.5 percent ever getting recycled).[32]

We pour **two million** tons of sewerage, industrial, and agricultural waste into our waterways every day.[33]

We have increased CO_2 levels by **40%** since the beginning of the industrial revolution.[34]

For everyone on the planet to live like the average American, we would require approximately **4.1 planet earths**.[36]

Between 1954 and 1994 we abandoned approximately **one-third** of all farm land due to it become too depleted to be commercially viable.[35]

THE BIRTH OF THE REAL-LIFE SUPERHERO

> "Life doesn't give us purpose. we give life purpose."
> —The Flash

Some time ago I was being interviewed about my book Create, Automate, Accelerate. The host finished the interview with a very random question,which caught me off guard: "Who is your favorite superhero, and why?"

This really threw me. I have watched a few Marvel movies, but have never read comics, and was never really drawn into the action hero world. I barely knew the most famous of characters, and certainly had no affinity to any.

Still, I was live, and I would look a bit foolish having no answer at all. I needed to come up with something, and fast. My answer surprised even me, and in many ways, led to the writing of this book. "Elon Musk," I replied. "For me, he risks everything to find solutions to help save humanity. He is a real-life superhero helping save millions of lives."

In retrospect, I am certainly not the first to make the link between Elon Musk and superheroes. He has been compared to Tony Stark, the face behind the Iron Man mask, on more than one occasion.

For those not familiar with Elon, he is the guy that co-founded PayPal, started Space X (the first private company to fly to space), and is a primary investor and CEO of Tesla Motors – the company that kick-started the electric vehicle market and is bringing solar and home energy storage to the masses.

However, it was a moment of clarity for me.

The world is in grave danger. The fate of humanity is uncertain at best. We need the X-Men to save us. But in the real world, X-Men are the average men and women who are fighting to find sustainable solutions to the world's problems.

And, just as with the X-Men, success will come by each person bringing his or her skills to the table and working collaboratively to find solutions together.

Superheroes think and act differently than most. They stand out from the crowd (especially those who choose brightly colored or glittery spandex as their fashion statement). They are not afraid to tackle what appears to be almost impossible odds. They focus on using their strengths, and adapt those strengths to address each challenge they face. They put the safety and wellbeing of others before their own needs. They save lives. And together (fingers crossed), they save the planet.

But most superheroes don't start out as superheroes. Something happens in their life. There is an awakening or transformation. A discovery of their power. A call to action. A breaking point where they realize life will never be the same.

The world is screaming for help. Whether you realize it or not, you do have an invitation and the power to answer that call. The question is, will you?

There is little doubt that what Elon has achieved during his life so far is way beyond average. He has done more to secure the future of sustainable transport than perhaps anyone dead or alive. However, he could not have done this alone, and alone he cannot fix all the world's problems.

Here is the problem though: even though Tesla make great cars (the Model S has been voted the best car ever made by more than one publication), they are still not "green". The plastic, metal, electronics, and transportation of the raw materials required to make each car, all contribute a little more to environmental collapse.

Elon needs help. A lot of help.

To make his car a genuinely green transportation solution, he needs to ensure that every part of the supply, distribution, and marketing chains are also operating sustainably. And right now, that is impossible.

Elon's superpowers are helping. But he needs more X-Men to join him and bring their powers to defeat climate change and global destruction. He is,of course, not alone in his quest, but the number of people currently fighting the good fight is not nearly enough.

Sounds a little dramatic? Maybe. But nowhere near as dramatic as the outcome if enough people do not step up and assist.

If you run a business that is committed to developing more sustainable products or services, or are educating consumers on how to make more sustainable choices, then you have joined the network of Real-Life Superheroes.

As the saying goes, if you are not part of the solution, you are part of the problem.

But why would so many people knowingly remain part of such a big problem? Perhaps one reason is best summed up by these words from poet Stanislaw Jerzy Lec: "No snowflake in an avalanche ever feels responsible." It is precisely this sentiment that causes such apathy amongst people—the belief that whatever harm they may be causing must be insignificant when looking at the size of the whole.

The birth of a superhero is perhaps the time when an average person realizes that he or she does matter and that he or she does make a difference. In this moment a transformation begins to unfold. The person can no longer continue as he or she was, hiding amongst a faceless crowd. While the person may not be quite ready to go shopping for a cape and mask just yet, the person know she or she must step forward, take responsibility, and begin to live life very differently.

Each day more and more people are crossing over and joining the socialpreneur revolution. Thanks to them, more solutions are becoming available to help increase the level of "greenness" with which we can operate our businesses.

Living with purpose and creating profit do not need to conflict with one another. Each day millions of dollars are being made by superhero entrepreneurs actively improving social and environmental sustainability.

Throughout this book, we will uncover solutions to many of the challenges we face. But they will only work if we all work together.

Every business does make a difference. It is up to you what type of difference you make with yours.

REAL-LIFE SUPERHERO PROFILE

Business Name: Patagonia.

Business Type: Adventure and travel clothing.

Founded By: Yvon Chouinard.

Year Established: 1973.

Mission: To build the best product, cause no unnecessary harm, and use business to inspire and implement solutions to the environmental crisis.

Powers: Support sustainable and cruelty-free farming practices, reduce reliance on petrochemical products, reduce impact from standard packaging, increase consumer awareness of bad clothing industry practices, contribute funds to community assistance, take care of employees and contract workers, and set new industry standards for others to follow.

The Story: Started in California by climber Yvon Chouinard, Patagonia began life as a division of Chouinard Equipment (which was founded in 1957 as a producer of climbing equipment). Due to some legal issues in 1989, Yvon sold off the climbing part of the business and focused on Patagonia, which he had started in 1973.

Around 1972 he became aware that the steel pitons his company sold, which at the time generated approximately 70 percent of its revenue, were responsible for harming climbing routes and the rock itself. Rather than ignore the problem, he developed chocks, a nonharmful alternative that for years served as the cornerstone of Chouinard Equipment's business.

In 1995 Yvon, after becoming aware of the harm caused by the intensive use of chemicals in growing conventional cotton, switched all his cotton sportswear production to organic cotton. This began Patagonia's commitment to sourcing only sustainable materials.

In 2001 Yvon co-founded an organization called "One Percent for the Planet," which encouraged businesses to give one percent of their sales to environmental causes. Patagonia led the way, and within the first ten years One Percent had helped raise over $100 million for environmental projects. To date, Patagonia alone has contributed $82M to grassroots environmental organizations.

Over the years, Patagonia's dedication to doing the right thing has established it as the industry standard in sustainable outdoor clothing, and for sustainable business practices in general. They recognize that there is still much work ahead, and continue to develop new and improved solutions for producing and distributing their products.

Website: www.patagonia.com

THE HERO'S JOURNEY

> "If you make yourself more than just a man,
> if you devote yourself to an ideal, you become
> something else entirely. a legend, Mr. Wayne."
>
> **—Alfred, Batman Begins**

Perhaps you have heard of "the hero's journey." It's an outline first identified by Joseph Campbell in 1949, that is found in storytelling, mythology, drama, and religion throughout the ages and from around the world. It provides a framework for the humble beginnings, growth, struggles, and ultimate success of a hero.

It also provides the perfect framework for anyone wanting to become a Real-Life Superhero (RLS). The following uses a simplified version put forth by Christopher Vogler in 2007.

Stage 1. THE ORDINARY WORLD: The hero begins in a normal world, which helps the audience identify with the character. As we join the story, the hero-to-be is usually facing some personal struggle or dilemma.

Almost every RLS starts their journey in a similar way. They are regular people facing the challenges of modern-day life. At this point, there is little to set them apart from anyone else.

Stage 2. THE CALL TO ADVENTURE: Something happens to make the hero aware of the possible conflict ahead. The seeds of change are planted.

For the RLS this may come in the form of some social media campaign, news report, or documentary that highlights some serious problem that causes them some emotional pain. It could also come from a personal experience, or influence from friends or family.

Stage 3. REFUSAL OF THE CALL: The hero shows his fear of the unknown and is likely to try to reject his or her role as a hero. The hero may question who he or she is to take on such a task.

The RLS feels much the same way. They fear what struggle, sacrifice, or failure may lay ahead. They are likely to make excuses or feel inadequate for the mission that lies before them. For many, this will include the struggle to avoid the temptation of chasing easy profits, or the criticism from peers for questioning the current status quo of the business world.

Stage 4. MEETING WITH THE MENTOR: The hero encounters a mentor or guide. This could be someone who has secret knowledge, or related skills and experience. This person helps provide the training, advice, equipment, and encouragement to prepare the hero for the dangers the hero will face.

The RLS also benefits from such a mentor. Someone to help provide support, industry knowledge, guidance, or useful contacts that can help the hero overcome the obstacles they face.

Stage 5. CROSSING THE THRESHOLD: At the end of the first act, the hero commits to his journey and leaves the "ordinary world." The quest has begun, and he or she is now in unfamiliar territory.

For the RLS this is the point that they mentally commit to making a difference, and start taking affirmative action. They will begin expanding their comfort zones and enhance their skills as they commence their new journey.

Stage 6. TESTS, ALLIES, AND ENEMIES: The hero faces a series of tests, and must forge alliances in his new world. They may also learn more about their enemy.

An RLS must do the same. They must form new friendships and connections to build the support network needed for success. They must also learn more about their enemy—what strengths do they have, and where are their weaknesses?

Stage 7. APPROACH: The hero and his newfound allies prepare for the big confrontation ahead and make their journey toward ground zero.

The RLS is likely to have a considerable journey ahead. There will be much preparation needed, and many obstacles to overcome before reaching their goals.

Stage 8. THE ORDEAL: Near the middle of the story, the hero must confront his or her greatest fears, or even death. From this confrontation he or she is profoundly changed and enters a new phase of life.

For an RLS this is usually a personal journey where they may need to face extreme financial stress, legal battles, loss, or fears such as public speaking, or overcome feelings such as rejection, inadequacy, or fear of failure. There is also a good chance they will, at some point, face the possible death of their vision or business. From this they become transformed into a new, more powerful and confident individual.

Stage 9. THE REWARD: At this point in the journey an epic battle ensues, and victorious, the hero finally takes possession of the treasure he or she has been seeking. Some celebration occurs, but danger still lies ahead.

The RLS will finally get the breakthrough they have been striving for and begin to see the light at the end of the tunnel. They will almost certainly celebrate their success so far. However, they still have a long way to go before their achievements make the full difference they want.

Stage 10. THE ROAD BACK: Into the third quarter of the story the hero makes his return journey to bring the treasure home. Often a chase will occur, which provides a reminder of the urgency, danger, and importance of the mission.

In the real world this will likely equate to the constant reminders of the social and environmental destruction occurring around them, and the pressure of making a business profitable before it collapses.

Stage 11. THE RESURRECTION: For the climax, the hero is tested one final time. He or she goes through a final transformation, but this time at a higher and deeper level. Through the hero's actions, the conflict that triggered the quest is finally resolved.

Most RLSs reach a point that for their product or service to reach market or be scaled, they must face a "last push." This final phase can be the most challenging, as much of the initial enthusiasm has been drained and they are exhausted from the long journey to reach this point. However, this final period lifts them to a whole new level of confidence and success, and the transformation to Real-Life Superhero is complete.

Stage 12. RETURN WITH THE ELIXIR: The hero returns home with newfound power and respect. The hero will often then embark on a new journey using his or her recently acquired skills, influence, and allies for furthering good in the world.

And so it is with the RLSs. They will continue the quest to save the world. Either through ensuring their project continues to deliver positive change or through creating new projects to provide new solutions in combating the enemies of social injustice and unsustainability.

It is also interesting to note that in all my years of studying Real-Life Superheroes in business, they never revert. That is, not a single one suddenly changes their mind and decides that building a socially responsible business is not for them and perhaps they should become an oil tycoon or open a sweat shop instead.

This should be a lesson for all of us. There are plenty of business owners that went from average Joe (or Josephine) focused on making money as a priority, to becoming a superhero and putting others before themselves. But you almost never, if ever, see the reverse.

Of course, unlike the movies, in the real world the journey outlined above can take years, not ninety minutes. The important point to remember, is that it is ordinary people just like you and me who are transformed by the journey of helping others.

Any internal struggle you may have in accepting this calling is normal. Resistance to the quest is normal. Denying your power is normal. None of these are evidence that you are not superhero material. They are merely an indication as to the current point of progress in your personal hero's journey.

As Jacque Fresco says, "If you think we can't change the world, it just means you're not one of those who will."

There are a few demons that may be blocking your path, which we must first slay before progressing further. So grab your weapon of choice (spare undies also recommended), and without further ado, let's begin . . .

"IF YOU THINK WE CAN'T CHANGE THE WORLD, IT JUST MEANS YOU'RE NOT ONE OF THOSE WHO WILL." - JACQUE FRESCO

THE DEMON OF DENIAL

> "Everyone wants to hear good news about their bad habits."
>
> —Dr. Pamela Popper

We live our earthly existence on a fine line between good and evil. (Again, a little melodrama, but you get the picture). On one side is our desire to help others and protect our species. On the other is selfish greed and a primal desire for self-preservation, dominance, and status within our tribe.

It is my belief, however, that most people are inherently good and want to do the right thing. My guess is, that includes you! Unfortunately, like most, you are probably sabotaging yourself from fully embracing your superhero identity and embarking on your mission to save the world.

Why and how do you manage to sabotage things so successfully despite the best of intentions? The answer to these questions can be complicated, but in part, it is thanks to the three internal Demons of Denial, Self-Justification, and Blame. In this chapter, we will look at the Demon of Denial, before moving on to the other two in more detail.

The Demon of Denial is a slippery beast that will keep you on your toes. He will try to seduce you with false information that you will want to believe, or distract you from seeing the truth.

For a long time, I was a climate change skeptic. Not a skeptic in the sense that I dismissed it as a hoax, but I was skeptical. I could see there were two sides to the debate, and both (on the surface) made sense. I allowed myself to believe too much of the anti-climate change propaganda because it felt better than admitting the truth. This allowed me to create just enough doubt around climate change that I did not worry too much or feel the need to do anything about it.

As I became more educated on the subject, looked at the evidence in detail, and questioned the sources of the information from both sides of the fence, I could no longer remain in denial.

And this is the trick to defeating the Demon of Denial: self-honesty, along with better education and the willingness to question sources of information. Take the time to properly research what is happening in the world and how your business plays a part in that. Be honest with yourself, and explore the unseen consequences and knock-on effects of your actions.

Beating denial is a painful process. It requires courage and perseverance. But it can be done.

THE DEMON OF SELF-JUSTIFICATION

> "Every villain is a hero in his own mind."
> —Tom Hiddleston

Psychologists have proven again and again that we are masters of justifying our actions, no matter how bad. Every type of crime, from the smallest to the largest,has been self-justified by someone. While Tom was only playing a villain (Loki), he makes an incredibly insightful observation. Villains see themselves as the hero, and the law as the enemy. Even Adolf Hitler believed he was doing the right thing, and serial killers justify their atrocities(at least in their own minds).So here's the sticky wicket of a dilemma: how would you know if you were batting for the bad boys, and not the good guys after all?

With the exception of a few war criminals and evil dictators, companies have been responsible for more deaths and human suffering than any mass murderer. Behind the glass doors and impersonal corporate branding sit individuals, collectively making decisions that lead to these deaths. Each one justifying their choices, which are thoroughly clouded by financial gain or increasing power and social status.

But you cry, "I am not a mass murderer or a corporate criminal." Maybe not, but I can almost guarantee you have made decisions that have contributed toward environmental collapse and quite probably (in its own small way) someone's death. And don't take this personally, we all have. And each one of us has justified those choices to ourselves.

I can already hear the violent backlash to these rather audacious opinions. So before you throw this book away in anger or despair, let me try to explain my seemingly harsh and extreme accusations. Let's take a look at a typical example we can all relate to:

If you bought low-cost clothing recently (personally or professionally),you have almost certainly, in a small way, contributed to death and destruction. And if you sell cheap clothing, you are a much larger cog in the war against humanity.

"Preposterous," I hear you cry. How so?

Perhaps the most notorious case is that of Rana Plaza, the Bangladeshi garment factory that collapsed, killing 1,136 people and injuring many more. But these were not the first nor the last deaths resulting from unsafe buildings and poor work conditions in textile manufacturing.

Thousands have died and millions more made sick as a consequence of the clothing industry's dismal pay, dangerous work conditions, and pollution. As Eileen Fisher(recipient of an environmental award, and a clothing industry insider) pointed out, "The clothing industry is the second largest polluter in the world . . . second only to oil."

So what does that have to do with you?

Probably, like me, you have heard of sweatshops and industrial pollution but have chosen to turn a blind eye. Sure, if a particular company is singled out in the media we may avoid their products for a while, but this is little more than a token gesture to a much larger problem.

If we do give some thought to the environmental and social injustice that is taking place, we self-justify our decision to buy cheap clothing because of the cost of more sustainable alternatives,or the lack of fashion choice. Often, we simply place blame on the companies producing these clothes.

The reality is that the large companies subcontract much of their manufacturing to Bangladesh and other developing countries. These factories are often forced to break laws and cut corners in order to save money. Not because they always want to, but because it is the only way they can compete for business.

The pressure from the large companies to reduce their costs is forcing them to run unethical businesses. Those same companies can only operate so long as we self-justify and then continue to giveth em our financial support anyway.

If you are buying discount clothing, then many corners are being cut to make sure you get that super low price. And it is not just discount clothing, many expensive brands do the same to increase their profits. The information and evidence are all around us. And, if we choose to justify our choices, that does not make the consequences any less real or our decisions any less impactful.

The good news is, there are alternatives.

Clothing companies such as Patagonia and Kathmandu have made real commitments to reduce their negative impact. They may not be the cheapest brands, but nor are they the most expensive. And the reason for their "realistic" pricing? They make sure workers get paid fairly and buildings are safe, and they source raw materials as sustainably as possible.

They are not perfect, but nor are they making excuses. They acknowledge the problems and have active programs to keep improving every dynamic of their businesses step by step.

You may use every excuse under the sun to justify your decision to buy cheap clothing. But once you know the truth and know of the alternatives, any reasons you come up with to buy from brands that are not working toward a sustainable future are little more than self-justification.

I don't mean to make you feel guilty or defensive. It's just that a superhero in training needs to be honest with themselves and with each other. We need to look past what is "normal" and see clearly through a haze of marketing-induced, emotional desires. Doing so is certainly not always easy, but as with any skill, you will improve with practice.

With each decision you make, check with yourself what compromises or sacrifices are made. Are your decisions being driven by personal gain at the expense of the world? Do they provide equal or greater value to the world than they cost it? Could you be making better choices and still make enough financially, or perhaps even more?

Every decision you make has some impact. You are responsible for each ripple or wave you create, even if you choose not to look. With this in mind, the superhero does their best to make the right decisions, even if it may reduce profit.

It does not matter what profession you practice or what industry you are in. Superheroes make decisions that put the world before themselves, and many are still paid well for doing so:

Superhero scientists and inventors are developing research and tech that provide better environmental solutions.

Superhero salespeople are persuading consumers to buy more sustainable products or services.

Superhero entrepreneurs and business owners are choosing to build more socially responsible companies.

Superhero support staff are wanting to work for companies they believe in, and support customers who have made sustainable choices.

Superhero marketers are focusing on helping sustainable businesses better educate the public.

Every position in every industry is crying out for superheroes to help. Check with yourself. What are you using your time and skills for?

Perhaps the most common self-justification for making poor or selfish decisions is money. Or more to the point, the fear of not having or making enough money. All too often there is an underlying limiting belief that an individual or company cannot afford to be more sustainable. It is easy to self-justify not buying sustainably produced clothing, organic food, or clean energy when "it is just too expensive." Yet it is often just as easy to self-justify buying the top-of-the-line phone, despite most people never needing more than a low- to mid-priced phone.

In the end, it is my belief, experience, and observation that those who commit to following superhero core values do just as well as those who don't. Maybe not immediately. But this is a part of the hero's journey. Remember, each hero is tested on his or her path. The question is, will you make sure your actions reflect your values and not your excuses?

THE DEMON OF BLAME

> "When you blame others, you give up your power to change."
> —Dr. Robert Anthony

Next we must face up to the Demon of Blame. This demon is a tricky one, but blame to an RLS is like kryptonite to Superman. In my book Create, Automate Accelerate, I explained how blame could read as

b-lame.

When we be-lame we become a cripple. So the moment we blame, we dis empower ourselves. Never a good move for any superhero!

The antidote to blame is simple in theory, harder in practice: learn to take responsibility. That does not mean something must have been "our fault," but that we assume responsibility. Then we actively find a solution to the problem.

As Winston Churchill said, "Sometimes we must do what is required." We can blame our suppliers, big corporates, governments, parents, society, employees, contractors, nature, or even God, but this will not change a thing. Taking responsibility and decisive action or finding a solution to your challenges will.

Within business, this attitude of taking responsibility can be very beneficial for the whole team. Much time and energy are wasted when people are trying to "find the person responsible." Doing so leads to a lot of discomfort, fear, and finger pointing. When you step up and take responsibility, it not only takes the pressure off others to get on and implement a fix, but it also sets a good example.

We don't like to admit it, but we all make mistakes at times, as will team members or suppliers. Worse still, somethings are just beyond our control. That's okay.

Jack Can field once described responsibility as "the ability to respond." Responding is precisely what a superhero does. When the Joker kidnaps a victim, Batman does not blame the victim for being in the wrong place, or the Joker for being a bad guy. He also knows the situation was not his own fault, but he responds anyway.

Kathmandu and Patagonia know it's not "their fault" that some employees in garment factories are underpaid, mistreated, or put in dangerous working environments. But they take responsibility to do something about it anyway.

As an RLS you must learn to catch yourself playing the blame game. Don't be hard on yourself when you do, we all blame from time to time—and don't be in denial! The trick is to see when you do it and then break the pattern. Stop being a victim of circumstance. Instead, strengthen your superpowers by becoming a master of responsibility and proactive change.

REAL-LIFE SUPERHERO PROFILE

Business Name: Ecostore.

Business Type: Household cleaning and hygiene products.

Founded By: Malcolm and Melanie Rands.

Year Established: 1993.

Mission: To build a significant and ongoing source of funding for nonprofit social projects, in an ethical and sustainable way.

Powers: Reduce poisons in our environment, improve consumer health, avoid animal products, reduce petrochemical waste in our environment, use carbon-negative packaging, increase consumer awareness, take care of employees, and fund community projects through the Fairground Foundation.

The Story: Started in New Zealand, Ecostore began with the desire to work on projects for social good, without the need to do fundraising. Malcolm considered several different business ideas, before finally deciding on cleaning products.

This business had the potential to meet both his financial needs for the nonprofit projects and to solve the (somewhat ironic) problem that we were polluting our bodies and environment each time we cleaned ourselves or our homes. Malcolm realized that we were not about to stop cleaning any time soon, so we needed alternatives that provided better solutions.

With nothing more than an overwhelming sense of purpose, (which he firmly believes is the most important starting point, and which must come through in everything you do), along with a NZ$30,000 loan from his brother, Ecostore was born. From the very beginning, he used three underlying principles to guide him:

1) Ethics comes first. He knew that to really sell his product, he must completely believe in it. He also understood this was

key to gaining the trust and respect of his customers. Ecostore is so strict, they reject at least fifty of the approved "eco" ingredients which many competitors still use, as they do not believe they are safe enough.

2) The product must be easy for the customer. Easy to buy and easy to use. This meant the products had to work in exactly the same way customers were used to. This principle also led him to go from selling via a mail-order catalog to selling through supermarkets and stores around the world.

3) It must be pleasurable. Therefore, packaging needed to look clean and professional. The products had to look like something the average person could trust, and not something that was brewed on a hippy commune. It was also important to make sure people felt good about their decision to buy the Ecostore brand.

By starting a company that focused on providing products that looked and worked like the ones people were already used to, and selling them at prices people were accustomed to paying, Malcolm made becoming more environmentally friendly an easy choice. Like with other superhero companies, it was not just about the raw product itself; the packaging, supply chains, and the way the company was operated were all optimized using superhero principles.

By taking a sustainability approach, they were able to go head-to-head with the large multi-billion- dollar companies who dominated the industry. (Imagine trying to take on Ariel or Tide based on "making your laundry whiter.")

It was not always easy. For the first several years every cent of profit was reinvested into the business. Even then this was not enough, and over time they needed to take on investment partners. But in the end, the determination and hard work paid off.

Ecostore has now spread to countries around the world and has helped reduce the negative impacts of millions of people each time they shower, clean the kitchen, or do their laundry.

And true to the original vision, Ecostore channels a percentage of its profits to the Fairground Foundation. Fairground is a nonprofit working to improve our communities in a variety of ways, which Malcolm now focuses on full time.

Websites: www.ecotstore.com and www.fairground.org

CHOOSING YOUR PATH

> "Heroes are made by the paths they choose,
> not the powers they are graced with."
> —Brodi Ashton

Once we stop our denial, self-justification, and blaming, we are free to forge a new path. We can escape the victim mindset, and we can avoid unintentionally becoming the villain. Instead we can choose to become the superhero. Indeed, heroes only ever become heroes as a result of the choices they make. So how do you identify the right path to follow?

While writing Create, Automate, Accelerate, I devised a framework I called "The 5 Ps of Priority." It was designed to help entrepreneurs ask the right questions in the right order to achieve the highest possible level of success.

Little did I know how much this very same framework was about to up heave my world. It has forced me to reevaluate my entire life, triggered a transformation, and forced me to accept a new mission that now lies ahead of me.

I am no superhero. Not yet anyway. But the 5 Ps of Priority triggered a shift that pushed me into stage five of the hero's journey, crossing the threshold. They helped me identify my superpowers and my role in the revolution. Sadly, it had little to do with the life I was trying to live at the time. Big change was needed.

I had heard it said," don't cling to a mistake just because you spent a lot of time making it." But it was not until this point that I began to appreciate its wisdom fully. So let me share with you the 5 Ps, and how they may help you too.

The 5 Ps – Purpose, Passion, People, Place, and Profit – are five questions that must be answered in the right order for an optimal result. Let's take a quick look at each and how you can apply this framework to design your business and your life.

First, we must identify your Purpose, or for the entrepreneur, the purpose of the business. For the RLS that purpose must be bigger than oneself. Ask yourself, what is your businesses core objective? Who will it help? Why does the world need it? How will it make people's lives better or improve the world in some way?

Every business should have a purpose beyond just making money. As Henry Ford said, "A business that makes only money is a poor business." Despite his more questionable side, Ford makes an important point. Having a purpose gives a business direction, helps motivate you, and will make any hard work far more emotionally rewarding.

This clarity of purpose leads to the second P, Passion. You need to find your passion in life. Each person has something they are skilled at and passionate about. It may be writing or numbers; perhaps it's sales or engineering. Whatever it is, it becomes a whole lot more interesting when purpose drives your passion.

We need to correct a very common misunderstanding about passion though. When most people talk about building a business or doing something you are passionate about,they usually use the word passion to infer "enjoy." But this is not the actual meaning of passion. Passion originates from the Latin word passio, which means "suffering." Even the modern definition of passion is "having intense emotion," and this intensity is certainly not always pleasurable.

I define passion in business (or in sport, or even relationships) as doing something you love and believe in so much that you are willing to suffer for it. Some days you may be "inspired," "in the flow," or "on fire." Others you will be afraid, stressed, disappointed, or angry,etc. You will suffer, and you will need to push yourself to the very edge to keep going. When you believe in what you are doing and believe in yourself, then you will be much closer to finding and experiencing real passion.

Very few, if any, projects worth doing can be done alone. We need the third P, People. Thankfully, because you now have purpose and passion, your enthusiasm becomes contagious. You will start to attract the right people to join and support your mission. The right people will bring essential skills or contacts that you may lack. They also bring extra time that you don't have, and provide support and encouragement when you need it. And you can be sure, you will need it at some point!

People also covers your customers. Identifying who they are, where they are, what their needs and expectations are, and figuring how you can best serve them. For the socially conscious business, we need to look to the expanded community too. How is our business impacting that community, and what can we do to support it?

With the third P clear,we can move to the fourth P —where is the best Place for the project? This will depend on what your business is and where the people are (both regarding team and customers). The answer to this question may already be obvious, but sometimes you may need to relocate, or base your operations in a different location to yourself.

The final P is Profit. How can you make your project financially viable? You need to do this so that you can pay your suppliers, team members, and yourself fairly. There are many ways to monetize a business, and you can use more than one. Although vital, this really should be the last question.

If you make profit your first priority, then the quality of the answers to the other questions are likely to become compromised, if they are ever considered at all. However, when you make purpose your priority, everything else will fall into place.

For those of you familiar with Maslow's hierarchy of needs, you will recognize that this is in effect designing your business from the top down. Many business gurus teach how to plan a business starting from the end and working back from there. And this is exactly what we are doing—only thanks to Maslow we realize that the money is not actually the end goal, something much larger is.

Many paths will provide financial stability, which will help us meet the bottom two levels of Maslow's pyramid (physiological needs and security). But many less will allow us to reach the highest three (love, self-esteem, and self-actualization). By using the 5 Ps of Priority you design a business that will meet all these needs.

So how did this realization disrupt my life?

In the original book (Create, Automate, Accelerate) I did not focus on the importance of social or environmental values regarding a business's purpose. Only that it should have a purpose of providing a product or service that met consumers' needs, and was driven by more than just making a profit.

To help promote the book I appeared as a guest on multiple podcasts and on several stages. Over time I found my presentation beginning to change. I realized that when I spoke about purpose and people, I was talking about much more than I had initially written about.

I began to preach the importance of socialpreneurship, the idea that our businesses should do more than just provide a good product or service,and that they should also have a positive social effect in the wider community.

And I genuinely believed what I was teaching. There was just one problem: my current businesses, and my life in general, did not reflect the level to which I was now encouraging others to live.

Don't get me wrong; I was doing my best to take care of my team and customers. I would not do anything that our society would consider immoral or bad. But I was not living close to my full potential to help save the world.

I began to understand David Attenborough's feelings when he asked, " How could I look my grandchildren in the eye and say I knew what was happening to the world and did nothing?"

No. I could not claim ignorance. And being "too busy" was a poor excuse. A dramatic change was needed.

I thought long and hard over how I could fix this dilemma. I had many ideas of how to improve my business or create new ones that could have a huge positive impact. But I realized my **purpose** was to help as many entrepreneurs and businesses as possible make the shift.

My **passion** is writing, teaching, sharing, and consulting. I love it. (Though I can assure you it still challenges me, and sometimes I find myself with writers' block, other times with fingers that can no longer type and eyes that feel like they are bleeding.) Writing is my lever. And so, the socialpreneur project was born. A whole new chapter in my life.

The project brings me into contact with amazing **people** that are a joy and inspiration to spend time with. It takes me to amazing **places**. And I am finding ways to monetize what I do, and to create a **profit** so I can keep on doing the work I love. And all the while, I am doing my bit to help save the world.

But enough about me . . . What about you? What's your purpose?

What is it that you want to improve or fix? How does (or will) your business make a positive difference to the lives of others? What changes need to be made in your industry to make it more sustainable? What can you do to help the revolution?

You cannot fix every problem in the world, nor do you need to. You are not alone. Instead, as the documentary Racing Extinction points out, you need to find "your one thing."[37] Then focus on that. (If you have not yet watched Racing Extinction, put it on your list of stuff to do this week.)

Do not expect to have the perfectly defined purpose overnight. With at least the outline of your purpose setting a direction, you can begin your journey. With no purpose at all, you are only drifting.

The only guideline is that your purpose should be bigger than yourself and for the greater good. Start by writing it down and refining it over the coming days, weeks, months, and even years. The "perfect" purpose, like anything, will start as a rough draft and then be improved over time.

To give an example, my purpose is,

Educate, encourage, and support business owners to develop more sustainable products and services that solve the world's current social, economic, and environmental challenges.

Some superheroes, such as Batman, try to focus on helping save their city. Others, like Superman, deal with challenges from the individual to the global. There is no right or wrong here. Everything is connected, and we all have our part to play.

We need people to help work on the big picture and on the small detail. We need Real-Life Superheroes that take care of their local community, and others that provide global solutions.

Don't be put off if you find other people are also trying to help solve the problems around that "one thing." Learn from each other and work with a spirit of cooperation and collaboration, not competition.

If you are not sure what your purpose is, find someone else who has already defined a purpose that you believe in, and then see what you can so to support them.

Now write yours. Take the time to read it each morning, refining it as inspiration strikes. And remember, wherever there is a problem, there lies an opportunity within its solution.

As The Flash reminds us, "One day your life will flash before your eyes. Make sure it's worth watching."

THE EMBLEM OF SOCIALPRENEURSHIP

> "Real worth requires no interpreter: its everyday deeds form its emblem."
>
> —Nicolas Chamfort

Every good superhero has some iconic look or logo to help brand them, and to represent their special powers or uniqueness. The socialpreneur superhero on the front cover of this book is no different. On his chest is the socialpreneurship logo that encapsulates the principles of a true socialpreneur and their socially responsible business.

Let me explain . . .

It is made up of four key elements: the light bulb, the plant, the arrow, and the superhero's shield. Each has a deep layer of symbolism and meaning.

The light bulb has long represented ideas and creativity. It also represents utility, accessibility, afford ability, technology, and commercial viability. The story of its invention also serves as a reminder to the importance of perseverance.

In addition to this, it shines alight to guide our way in the darkness and provides light to nurture the plant.

The plant itself represents the environment which is not only nurtured but also protected by technology (in this case, the bulb). The plant also represents growth and the future. Here there is a synergy between technology and nature.

Another facet of the plant is health. In this case the health of our team, our customers, the entire human race, and the planet. Plants can also provide renewable raw materials.

The arrow provides direction, recycling, sustainability, and the idea of moving forward (progress).As it loops back around it shows a reconnection to our past and the ancient knowledge we had so we could live in harmony with nature. It brings that wisdom into the present day and teaches us to integrate it as a part of technology.

The shield is the symbol of protection. In the context of the superhero, it also represents the concept of integrity, defending the innocent, putting others first, social justice, and freedom.

The shield reminds us to have the courage and confidence to keep fighting for good, no matter how bad the odds. And, those who wear it are willing to stand out from the crowd and dare to be different.

The green stands for nature, the environment, balance, harmony, and tranquility. It is also the color of money, showing they do not always need to be in conflict.

The white is the color of cleanliness and purity. It helps remind us to be both ethical and environmentally clean.

If all entrepreneurs and businesses adopted this emblem and the principles it embodies, then I think the world would be a very different place. I encourage you to contemplate it and use it to help guide you in the tough decisions ahead. Let it help forge a new identity for you and your business.

If you want to remind yourself regularly of the principles and ethics of being a socialpreneur, then go to the member's area for this book and grab yourself a free screensaver of the socialpreneurs emblem, or pickup one of the socialpreneur Real-Life Superhero tee-shirts: www.ethicallymad.com/superheroes.

REAL-LIFE SUPERHERO PROFILE

Business Name: Aperia Technologies

Business Type: Automatic tire inflation technology for commercial vehicles

Founded By: Josh Carter and Brandon Richardson

Year Established: 2010

Mission: To uncover compelling opportunities, reveal creative technology solutions, and make clear the fact that we can "change the world, one revolution at a time."

Powers: Increase fuel efficiency of commercial vehicles, increase life expectancy of tires, reduce accidents caused by tire blowouts, increase customer awareness of simple ways to reduce their carbon footprint, increase employee sustainability awareness through initiatives to reduce office and operational impact.

The Story: Aperia was founded at Stanford by two entrepreneurial engineers in 2010. By 2011 they already had the first field trial in place, and over the following two to three years they refined their invention. By 2014 they had a commercial product, and by 2015 it had been adopted by over one hundred commercial fleets.

So, what is it that Aperia makes exactly? And why do they deserve superhero status?

Josh and Brandon have created a very cool little device that can be fitted to commercial vehicles (trucks, trailers, tractors, etc.) in just five to ten minutes. It helps keep tire pressure at optimal levels, thus reducing CO_2 levels thanks to better fuel efficiency; increases the life expectancy of tires (reducing wastage and costs); and increases safety.

But it is not just the product itself that makes them superheroes. They have put a lot of effort into ensuring their company also operates as efficiently and sustainably as possible. Here are just a few of the strategies they have implemented in their workplace:

- They have provided an electric/hybrid charging unit for employees.

- They recycle their signage.

- They have fitted lighting occupancy sensors to reduce power usage.

- They have fitted solar screening on windows to reduce power used for cooling.

- They have installed an efficient heating unit and insulated the warehouse.

- They have designed the office to use only digital documentation.

- They have designed the office to use natural lighting.

- Office and warehouse furniture and equipment have been made from recycled materials.

- They are located near two major public transportation lines to encourage public transport use.

- They provide regular sustainability and safety training for staff.

Aperia's product demonstrates that you can create a profitable company by creating products that help make the world just that bit more sustainable, and their operational approach shows you can save money while becoming more sustainable. Indeed, they report that the heating improvements alone save over $1,000 per year, while power management strategies save another $1,000 plus annually.

Websites: www.aperiatech.com

JOINING FORCES

Once you too have crossed the threshold (stage five of the hero's journey), the next step in becoming an RLS is to forge alliances.

In my last book (Leveraging Masterminds), I pointed out that the greatest achievements of mankind were never made by an individual, but always by groups of people. This is true even when one or two individuals may get all the credit.

Many high-profile people throughout history, including Einstein, J.R. R.Tolkien, and Henry Ford, belonged to a mastermind group. Each may have received much of the fame, but it was their participation in these groups that proved crucial to their achievements.

If you are serious about changing the world, you will need support. You may need the help of people with skills or experience that you don't have. Maybe you need investment capital or new connections. Perhaps you will need emotional support, encouragement, or guidance.

Chances are, you will, at some point, need all the above.

Equally, you will want to avoid spending too much time with those who have a negative attitude toward your objectives. Another great aphorism that has stuck with me is, "Stay away from negative people. They have a problem for every solution."

To be clear though, negativity is not the same as recognizing challenges or obstacles to overcome. Someone who sees problems you have not but believes the end goal is possible, and helps you get there, is entirely different from a naysayer who just thinks the destination is impossible or a waste of time. You need the former. You need to ditch the latter.

Look for other like-minded individuals, online and offline, to connect with. You may find them in forums, blogs, or chat rooms. You could find them in local meet up groups, associations, or at seminars. My advice is to search high and low and make as many connections as you can. And the sooner, the better.

This book will go on to help give some practical advice you can implement to reduce your environmental footprint while minimizing costs and increasing revenue. But it is only a book. There is no way it can cover every unique set of circumstances or predict every breakthrough in technology that may assist you. This is why, having solid network of collaborators and supporters around you will make all the difference.

They can help keep you up-to-date on new developments, offer an outside perspective, share their expertise, and connect you with others who may be critical to your success.

As you may have guessed, I am a fan of mastermind groups—that is,when formed with the right people and conducted in the right way. I won't go into detail here, but I do suggest that you make a point of joining or starting one as soon as possible.

For resources on mastermind groups and other networks that could prove useful, check out this book's member's area at www.ethicallymad.com/superheroes.

TWO MORE DEMONS TO FACE

> "If you correct your mind, the rest of your life will fall into place."
> —Lao Tzu

We have identified the Demons of Denial, Self-Justification, and Blame. We now face two more: the Demon of False Logic and its Siamese twin, the Demon of False Economy. Beware, both these demons are BFFs with the Demon of Self-Justification!

If there is anything history has proven, it is that we have a fascinating ability to delude ourselves. We can often see this in others, but we are so good at self-delusion we are virtually blind to it within ourselves. So of course, this chapter won't apply to you ;-)

One of the ways in which we reinforce this delusion is with our ninja skills in false logic. Sometimes we will use false logic to help self-justify something; other times we are simply too lazy, or incapable of seeing the truth. In his book You Are Not So Smart, David McRaney exposes just how susceptible we are to false logic. A truly insightful read, and well worth the time for any superhero in training.

One common false logic justification for many unsustainable choices is "other people are worse than me." The logic here being that if others are worse, I am better, and therefore what I do is okay. Obviously this rationale is flawed; otherwise, every criminal would be doing nothing wrong, so long as they were not the worst criminal.

Another very common excuse based in false logic is that something is "normal." If you ever catch yourself using the"N word," ask the nearest person to slap you hard with a wet fish.(Proverbially speaking, that is. I don't endorse mistreatment of fish!) Superheroes are not normal, and proud of it.

Normal is relative to time and place. It is not an absolute. Slavery was normal. Witch hunts were normal. Remaining normal by whatever accepted standard of the day prevents progress and is hardly an accurate measure of what is right.

In today's world, our perception of what is normal is now more distorted than ever. Never in history have we eaten many of the foods that we eat today. Never have we destroyed the environment at the rate we do today. Never have we poured as many chemicals on our skin as we do today or surrounded ourselves with as many electromagnetic frequencies, used as much plastic, spent countless hours on social media, or many of the other things we do today that we consider "normal." Justifying decisions or actions on the grounds of being normal is weak logic indeed.

While it may be easy on the outside to see the weakness in these arguments, I am sure almost all of us have used them at some point. This is particularly so when it comes to decisions that will make us more money or get us what we want.

Despite the flawed logic, when we use an excuse like this, we usually believe it. If we did not, then we would have to admit to being a weak person, or worse, wrong. And none of us likes to do that! As Lao Tzu explains, "Mastering others is strength; mastering yourself is true power." As a superhero, you need to develop your power more than your strength.

Here's a thought experiment for you: imagine artificial intelligence is now in control. Its job is to protect the planet and preserve the human race. To do this, it must ensure that all business activity is socially and environmentally sustainable. If not, the owners of any offending business are to be removed from society. Do you have reason to be worried? This scenario may be a little extreme, but if you play along and are honest with yourself, you will begin to expose many of your personal excuses. (And we all have them.)

There will always be someone doing more harm than you or setting some bad example. That is not an excuse to copy them. There are also plenty of people setting good examples and making better decisions.

It just depends on who you choose to spend time with or compare yourself to.

How about the mother of all false logic self-justifications, "If I don't do it, someone else will." Regardless of whether this is true or not, it hardly makes it right.

Sometimes false logic leads to false economy. Take for example the decision to upgrade to an electric vehicle. Electric cars produce far less CO_2 than petrol, no argument there. But does that mean you should make the switch?

Well, maybe . . .

The embodied energy, levels of CO_2 emitted, and amount of pollution generated in making an EV is greater than you are likely to produce driving your existing petrol car for many years to come.

So if you are using the logic that you are being more "eco-friendly" or saving money on fuel by changing your car, then you are using false economy. The best thing for your wallet and the environment is to keep the gas guzzling beast you have. At least for now.

If your car is packing its final sad and needs replacing, then, yes, an EV is almost certainly the right choice.

Another example is that of paper versus plastic bags.

The obvious answer is that paper is better than plastic. But the truth is not always so obvious. Paper is weaker and requires around six times the raw material to produce a single bag. Trees maybe better than oil, but they still come at a cost. And paper in a landfill produces methane, which is far more potent as a greenhouse gas than carbon dioxide. In most cases paper is worse than plastic from a carbon perspective, but at least it does not choke sea life. The reality is that paper versus plastic is not a black-and-white argument. The answer is complicated and will depend if your priority is protecting sea life or protecting forests and preventing climate change.

These demons of false logic and false economy make things tricky when trying to make the right decisions. Like any of the demons though, being conscious of them is an essential first step in overcoming them.

Researching the facts and getting multiple opinions are also important strategies in defeating these particular demons. Try to seek as many diverse perspectives as possible.

Be sure to listen carefully to opposing opinions. When we ask the opinion of someone who thinks and believes the same as we do, we are not seeking genuine feedback—just self-validation. By listening to the opposition, we can better find the weakness in our thinking. Challenging our thoughts not only helps produce better solutions, but may also prevent us from following ideas that could have unseen consequences.

MEET YOUR ARCHENEMY

> "The enemy is fear. We think it is hate; but it is really fear."
> —Mahatma Gandhi

We have faced five demons that will challenge you in your quest to save the world. But there is one super-villain who controls them all. He is also the most famous: Fear.

Fear takes many forms, and like in any good superhero story, you will face this archenemy on more than one occasion. Here are just a few of his most familiar forms:

- Fear of losing money or current security

- Fear of what others will think

- Fear of not being skilled enough for the mission

- Fear of failure

- Fear of ridicule

- Fear of not being able to make enough money

- Fear of not getting the support you need

- Fear of being overwhelmed

- Fear of missing out on something else

- Fear of success and the change it will bring

- Fear of financial or social responsibility

- Fear of having to make sacrifices

- Fear of rejection by peers, friends, family, or society

- Fear of intimidation

Few people, if any, are fearless. When you read the biography of many great people throughout history, you find a consistent theme: they were, at times, afraid. Their successes were possible, not because they were fearless, but as a result of learning to manage their fears.

Many superheroes wear underwear on the outside because it is a convenient way to carry a spare pair—in case of emergencies!

All too often a "could have been" superhero ends up beaten by fear. This is, of course, a tragedy for not only the individual but also for society. Franklin D. Roosevelt once said, "The only thing we have to fear is fear itself," and this is certainly true if the fear is preventing us from living life to its full potential.

Fear is a particularly powerful super villain. One of his superpowers is the ability to make himself almost invisible, and another is mind control. If you are brave enough to look, you will often find fear hiding under the guise of a "good reason."

When you give reasons (make excuses) why you can't do something, look to see if it is fear making the decision for you. The fear is not always easy to see; even the strongest and most experienced of superheroes can be tricked at times.

This is when having allies can be a huge help. Good friends, business partners, or members of a mastermind group may be able to unmask fear by looking from an outside perspective. Another useful technique which many superheroes use to battle this enemy successfully is meditation. It helps provide a level of clarity and insight that is almost impossible to achieve when we are caught up in the day-to-day management of our business.

To help manage fear, it is good to gain a better understanding of exactly what it is. You may have seen fear described as the following:

Future Expectations **A**ppearing **R**eal

While this is true, technically excitement could be described in the same way. In fact, the difference between fear and excitement is subtler than most people realize. Both are about future events, both release adrenalin, both get felt in the stomach, and most importantly, both can influence your decisions.

The only real difference is that fear causes you to see a negative future reality, and excitement a positive one. If unchecked, fear can drive you away from your goals,while excitement pushes you toward them.

There are many books written on this subject alone, and I suggest you read a couple so that you know your foe intimately inside and out.

Like most villains, fear is not pure evil, and even has its good side, as well as its bad side.

Sometimes, such as when a lion is chasing you across the savanna, fear has a very real purpose in protecting you. More often though, it does not. Part of your superhero training will be to identify fear, understand fear, and then learn when to listen to it and when to ignore it.

It saddens me to think how many lives are wasted due to fear. How many people want to do the right thing, but ignore their calling because they are scared? As the Green Hornet explains, "It's not dying that you need to be afraid of, it's never having lived in the first place."[38]

What is the worst that happens if you try and fail? But what if you could have made a difference, but never tried?

I urge you to ask yourself why you are not doing more to help save the world. Whatever the reason, I can almost guarantee that if you dig deep enough, you will find fear hiding in your answer. It may not be obvious, but it is almost always there.

Are you worried that your business won't be competitive enough? Are you afraid that you will miss some other opportunity that will make you more money? Are you concerned the market is not yet ready and there won't be enough demand for a more sustainable product or service?

Once you have shone a light on your fear,it begins to lose some of its power and allows you to work on defeating it. There are a variety of methods in overcoming fear, and I suggest mastering one or two of them. NLP (neuro-linguistic programming), EFT (Emotional Freedom Techniques), and hypnosis are three very popular techniques that have proven effective for many people.

There are plenty of free online courses teaching these better than I ever could in the space of this book. Checkout the resource area where I provide some links for you if you are interested: **www.ethicallymad. com/superheroes.**

My final suggestion is to get backup. Surrounding yourself with the right type of people will be a recurring theme throughout this book. Good emotional support can help give you strength to make tough decisions. Equally, avoiding the wrong kind of people is also important. Try to stay away from, or at least spend much less time with, those who reinforce your fears (or those who encourage you to put profit before principle).

REAL-LIFE SUPERHERO PROFILE

Business Name: Arkin Tilt Architects

Business Type: Architect

Founded By: Anni Tilt, AIA and David Arkin, AIA, LEED AP

Year Established: 1997

Mission: To design beautiful, inspiring, energy-efficient buildings using low-impact materials, which are better for the environment and health.

Powers: Reduce waste, minimize the use of unsustainable materials, reduce health issues caused by toxic building materials, reduce energy requirements through better design, create better awareness of sustainable design and material use, and further the use of photosynthetic and renewable materials that can sequester carbon and diminish the overall CO2 footprint of buildings.

The Story: Anni and David started their architectural firm with the belief that architecture should be a marriage of good design and green priorities.

By employing passive solar design principles and choosing better materials they could design buildings to require less artificial light, heating, and cooling. This reduces not only operational costs, but also the buildings' carbon footprint. With careful study of weather and ecosystem data, each building responds to its specific site conditions, creating a natural fit to its climate and circumstances.

They also understood that many standard materials cause harm to the health of their occupants. In a commercial building, this health issue can cost businesses money in lost productivity and increased health insurance premiums. By designing buildings with more natural materials, they can ensure construction will not only be nontoxic, but also more environmentally sustainable: better for the companies that used the buildings, better for the people working in them, and better for the world at large.

Furthermore, like most superheroes, designing a better product or service was not good enough. They also wanted to ensure that their company reflected the same values and ideas.

And so, they encourage staff to bicycle to work, operate low office waste initiatives, and use solar power. They also encourage team members to get involved with volunteer work, and do many pro bono projects for organizations they believe can make a positive difference, but which otherwise couldn't afford their services.

They also do a lot of work to help raise awareness about more sustainable materials and design at both a professional and a consumer level. They are also among the co-founders of the California Straw Building Association (CASBA) and David currently serves as its Director.

Their efforts have not gone unappreciated. Since 1997 they have received awards for design, business, and sustainability almost every single year—most years more than one.

Websites: www.arkintilt.com, www.strawbuilding.org

THE ENEMY HIDING IN PLAIN SIGHT

> "The cause is hidden; the effect is visible to all."
> —Publius Ovidius Naso (Ovid)

There is another enemy we must face that is everywhere we look. From the houses we live in and the food we eat, to the clothes we wear and the cars we drive. It even permeates every electric vehicle, solar panel, and sheet of recycled paper.

This enemy is best known as embodied energy.

She is all of the accumulated energy required to produce any product or service. The energy that is used to mine or grow the raw materials, and the energy required for manufacturing, packaging, storage, and transportation.

When you expand this out, you can start can start to get a sense of the problem. Even this book required energy to make: the computer I am typing on, the chair for me to sit on, the desk to write at, power to operate the computer, energy to transfer the data during my research, etc.

While much of this embodied energy is shared among the many products or services that I create, it all adds up. And this is before the book is even ready for distribution. Then more energy is required for the book to be printed, or read on a digital device.

We are never going to eliminate embodied energy. It is (at least to our current understanding of physics) impossible. However, we can consciously reduce our energy consumption and ensure that the power we do use comes from renewable sources.

For example, in some countries, you can choose a power company that buys only renewable energy. You could switch to an electric vehicle to deliver your products or to meet clients. You can become more proactive at finding ways to reduce energy usage in your office. In later chapters, we will look at more specific ways to address these challenges on a practical level.

Remember, the embodied energy in your products and services is an accumulation of the operation of your business (equipment, staffing travel, energy usage,etc.), The supply chains you use, the supply chains your suppliers use, and so on.

Until, as a planet, we make the switch to 100 percent renewable energy for all our energy needs and stop using limited resources that can't be recycled, we will never be truly sustainable.

The good news is this transformation has already begun.

But for it to be effective we need every business owner and consumer to be aware of the choices they are making. We need to accept that sometimes we may need to put the planet before our profit margin and make a little less money for the sake of our future. Other times there is no conflict at all, just an informed conscious decision.

We will not conquer this enemy overnight, but starting today we can begin to disarm her.

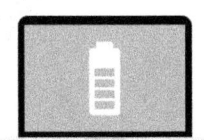

Embodied energy makes up approx. **70%** of a laptop's energy use over its lifetime
(**30%** from operating it).[39]

Carbon footprint of **stainless steel** is **6.15 kg** per 1 kg.[31]

Embodied energy in a VW Golf A3 is **18,000 KWH.**[40]

Carbon footprint of **aluminum** is **8.24 kg** per 1 kg.[31]

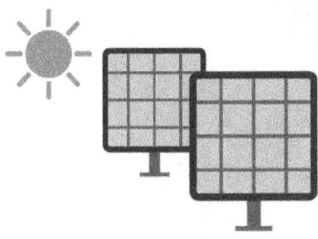

Embodied energy in 1m2 of monocrystalline photovoltaic cell (solar panel) equals **4750 MJ**, or approx. **242 kg CO_2.**[41]

Carbon footprint of **hard cheese** is **12 kg** per 1 kg.[44]

The carbon footprint of an **iPhone 5S** before ever using it is **56.7 kg.**[42]

Carbon footprint of a **27-inch iMac** is **505 kg.**[43]

THE GREAT LIE THAT MAY DESTROY THE WORLD

> "The light you see at the end of the tunnel is the front of an oncoming train."
>
> —David Lee Roth

The easiest lie to fall for is the one you want to believe. It is time to examine one of the most seductive lies of them all.

I have spent a lot of time reading, believing, and even at times teaching personal development philosophy. A common phrase you often hear in these circles is, "If it is not growing, it is dying." This sentiment is certainly shared by most economists, business owners, and governments.

But is it true? And worse, might striving for continued growth actually be killing us both metaphorically and literally?

The idea that growth can be as dangerous as it can beneficial is a concept that most business owners and politicians do not want to hear and certainly don't want to believe.

Unfortunately, trying to maintain never-ending economic growth is the net result of combining extreme greed, unbelievable stupidity, and a lot of wishful thinking. No society has ever achieved it, though many have tried. The Roman, Ottoman, Mongol, Persian, Han, and British, amongst others, have all managed to rise to great heights, but each of these great empires has eventually collapsed.

As individuals, investors, and business owners we all want to believe we can continually increase our profits. And while this is understandable, is there perhaps a darker side we are failing to see?

Skeptical? Ask an oncologist about growth. They understand all too well about the destructive potential of unlimited growth. There is nothing in nature that is able to sustain infinite growth. Only the universe itself continues to expand, and many scientists believe even this has its limits.

In biology, this growth limit potential is known as the carrying capacity. That is, the maximum number of individual organisms that can be sustained by a given environment. Any restrictions,which include physical space and resources such as food, are known as environmental resistance.

In the case of cancer, the tumor will continue to grow until it kills its host—therefore limiting its growth and inevitably causing its demise. Is it any wonder then that many experts have likened the human species to being a cancer on planet Earth?

From a business perspective, we have similar growth restrictions. These limits are defined by the number of potential customers, available raw materials, capacity of distribution, etc. In both nature and business, the carrying capacities are not fixed, but defined by many fluctuating variables.

There are a lot of personal development gurus preaching the law of abundance. And while I do believe we have plenty for all, I do not think that gives permission for excessive greed or removes the consequences of taking without proper resource management.

For centuries the native peoples of Alaska lived in harsh conditions but had little problem surviving due to their expert hunting skills and a plentiful resource of whales, walrus, and other wildlife. During the 1800s everything changed. Whalers and trappers began arriving en masse. They took everything they could find, and within fifty years the once abundant food supply had become so depleted that the local Inuit began to starve.

Sadly, this is far from a unique story. It has been repeated again and again around the world. Businesses exploit an area of its natural resources and leave the locals to suffer while the business owners become wealthy. Is this proof of infinite abundance and the potential for unlimited growth for all?

Sustainability is grounded in proper resource management, not infinite or unrestricted growth. That does not mean growth is bad; it just means that using growth as the primary metric to measure a company's success is very dangerous indeed.

In days gone by, the carrying capacity of an individual business was relatively low compared to the possibilities of today. For example, a blacksmith in a small town had a limited number of customers he could reach and a limited production capacity.

The number of blacksmiths that could stay in operation within a single town was defined in part by the size of the town. If the town grew, a blacksmith could either expand his business, or someone would move in to fill the excess demand. While there has always been wealthy and poor, this relatively low potential for a business's carrying capacity (and therefore its size) created a moderate degree of wealth distribution.

Then globalization occurred.

Through technology, it became possible for companies, and now even individuals, to meet the demands of millions. They can grow way beyond previous limits. And most "developed" societies even support and encourage this. We celebrate their huge financial success, but what is the true cost to society?

Granted, it has brought some benefits. Companies have been able to amass large amounts of money that give them the ability to invest in the development of new technologies and scale production to reduce costs. However, this system has also allowed the growth of wealth in a small minority while increasing pressure and debt on the majority.

More and more industries are dominated by a small handful of players, and thanks to technology, they are able to fulfill more customers with less and less staff. This means that fewer companies are required to meet any given demand.

Take for example Uber. Uber has been responsible for putting enormous pressure on traditional taxi drivers. Not just in Uber's local city, nor their country, but on a global scale. Due to cheaper rates, consumers have seen this as a good thing. But is it?

For a start, Uber has been running with massive losses (Bloomberg estimates $1.2 billion in the first half of 2016 alone), a common strategy for venture capital funded start-ups. Because they have large amounts of investor money, they can operate for years without making a profit—something almost all their competitors are unable to do. This allows them to dominate, but is financially unsustainable in the long term. Once they own the market, they must increase their prices, and the average consumer will be back to paying close to the original price, only now with fewer service providers to choose from.

The impact that Uber is having will only worsen in the coming years as it begins to roll out its autonomous driving vehicles. When this happens, millions of drivers' incomes will disappear, with much of the cash going to a small group of already wealthy investors.

This approach is also pushing more and more people out of work or forcing them to work on the breadline to remain competitive. Pushing people to the financial edge is rarely good for society. The repercussions are well known; increased poverty all too often leads to increased crime, decreased education, and decreased health.

Don't get me wrong. The system has not collapsed—yet. But we need to acknowledge that the limits of corporate and individual economic growth have never been this unrestricted. We are in the midst of conducting a global economic experiment that many would argue is destined to crash more spectacularly than any of the great empire demises to date.

If companies and private individuals continue to hoard wealth beyond their needs, then a tipping point will be reached. This may be avoided if they use their wealth to reinvest into ongoing development, fixing ALL the damage they cause (not just token gestures to improve brand image) and taking proper care of the people that make up the entire company (rather than avoiding responsibility, avoiding taxes, and giving insanely large bonuses to a handful of select individuals).

As a Real-Life Superhero and business owner, you will need to address these moral challenges as you become increasingly successful. Do you continue to self-justify, or do you find ways to ensure fair distribution of resources to your community?

Common arguments (self-justifications):

"But other people have more than me."

"There is plenty for everyone"(despite all the evidence).

"Others can do the same if they want to."

"It's legal. If it were a problem, then it would not be allowed."

"If I don't do it, someone else will."

"I worked hard for it; I deserve to keep it all."

"If my company is not growing, it is dying."

"We can't risk being eaten by the competition."

"Growth is our responsibility to our shareholders."

Some of these arguments may be technically correct. But they do nothing to prevent the limits of carrying capacity or the social implications of unrestricted greed (I mean growth).

Knowing that we need growth but also that too much growth is not a good thing, we end up facing at ruly difficult question: what is a fair or sustainable amount of growth?

I certainly don't have the answer, as it is incredibly complex and far from black or white. The one thing I can be sure of however, is that those businesses who experience substantial growth have an equally, if not exponentially, increased responsibility to manage the result of that growth (both in terms of profit and influence).

As a society, we may eventually need to readdress the entire structure of the economic system. We need to realize that many of the limitations that have prevented this type of unprecedented growth in previous centuries, no longer apply. The potential repercussions of this are scary, to say the least.

Struggle, famine, rebellions, and war are already the reality for millions. If we are a genuinely intelligent species, then let's figure how to avoid this from escalating further before the proverbial shit really hits the fan.

As individuals, as businesses, and as a society, we must learn to create balance. We must grow enough to become sufficiently strong; then, rather than trying to outdo everyone else, we must assist others in becoming as strong as us. And, to ensure that cooperation is not lost to competition.

Bob Dylan offers an important observation to those taking the hero's journey: "A hero is someone who understands the responsibility that comes with his freedom." This wisdom is especially important as one reaches financial freedom. It is not how much money you make that defines you as a hero. It is how you made that money and what you choose to do with it that counts.

We need to look beyond the profit and loss statements of a business,and instead look at what service or benefit the business provides to society. How does it re-invest in improving its industry? How does it take care of its employees? How does it give back and look after the communities it touches? How does it help the planet as a whole?

LEARNING TO THINK LIKE A SUPERHERO

> "There is a right and a wrong in the universe,
> and that distinction is not hard to make."
>
> —Superman

To act like a superhero, you must first learn to think like a superhero. Obviously easier said than done, but I will try to share a couple of strategies that may help.

The most important point to re-emphasize is that Real-Life Superheroes make decisions that are driven by the greater good, and they are foremost solution finders—not excuse makers.

To get better results, you need to ask better questions. Firstly, we must start by asking questions that create better awareness.

Here are a few to get you started:

What raw materials do our products or services depend on? How are they sourced? What is the environmental impact in producing them?

How much energy do we use, both in terms of electricity and fuel for transport? How is this being produced? What are the consequences of this production?

Who are our suppliers? What are their environmental and social policies?

How are our goods or services transported? What is the impact of this transportation?

What waste is being produced either by us or by our customers because of our product or service? What happens to that waste? What are the environmental impacts that waste has?

What equipment do we use? What was the environmental and social impact caused by the manufacturer producing that equipment?

What is the impact our business has on our employees, our community, our country, and on the world?

Taking the time to do a little research will create a lot of awareness. You are no doubt already subconsciously aware of a lot of it, but bringing it to the surface is an essential first step if we are going to do something about it.

Before writing this book, I thought I had a decent understanding of what was happening in the world. It is, after all, what motivated me to start writing it in the first place. But the more I dug deeper, the more I realized how little I actually knew. And the more I discovered, the more I became motivated to do something.

Throughout the book, I will include some of what I learned. But there is no way to cover it all. I encourage you to go to the online resource section for this book and study some of the suggested resources. Share them with your team too, and get them involved in helping you answer the questions above.

A superhero can't begin to save the world if he is not sure exactly what needs saving. With a greater level of awareness, you will start to see what can be done to improve things. There is so much we can already do, and increasingly better solutions come to market every day.

Next, the proactive questions. Following are a few examples of good questions you can try asking yourself, and your team, to help get you thinking like a solution-finding RLS:

What would be the most important thing the business could do to reduce its negative impact on society or the environment? How might we achieve that?

What can we do to lessen the amount of power we use? Are there any other forms of energy we could use that have a less negative impact?

Which service providers could we change to reduce our business's indirect footprint?

What products or services could we offer that would help reduce the effects of climate change, pollution, or social inequality?

What can we do as a business to support our local community?

Becoming a sustainable business is not something that just happens at the flick of a switch. World champion martial artists don't just read a single book, practice the moves once or twice, and then go on to win. They put the theory into practice repeatedly over time, until eventually they master it. The theory has become unconscious instinct. And so it is for the Real-Life Superhero.

You will need to research and improve continually. In the beginning it will take conscious effort, just as with learning any new skill. But over time it will become more and more automatic, like a natural reflex. Just be patient with yourself early on, and don't be too hard on yourself when you slip up. Learn from your mistakes and aim to do better next time.

"TACKLING CLIMATE CHANGE IS THE BIGGEST ECONOMIC OPPORTUNITY IN THE HISTORY OF THE US." - LEONARDO DICAPRIO

PART 2:
STRATEGIES FOR WAR

"All the best heroes are ordinary people
who make themselves extraordinary."

—Gerard Way

RULES OF THE GAME

> "Rules are for the obedience of fools
> and the guidance of wise men."
> —Douglas Bader

Like any good hero, you will need to have a set of rules that you can fall back on. These rules will provide some simple guidelines that allow you to design strategies to overcome the obstacles you will face on your mission.

These rules are intended to guide us toward the development of sustainable businesses and a sustainable society. This ideal was defined best by three-term Norwegian prime minister, Gro Harlem Brundtland, when she explained that sustainable development is "development that meets the needs of the present without compromising the ability of future generations to meet their own needs."[45]

The rules are quite simple and are the foundation of everything else that follows. Their essence can also be found at the heart of many martial arts philosophies, and give us the famous three Rs of reduce, reuse, and recycle.

1) **Reduce.** Most martial arts teach the best solution is to avoid combat in the first place. If you can avoid fighting in the first place, then no one will get hurt. Wisdom for the RLS eco-warrior indeed.

    If we can avoid buying, using, or creating something that is unnecessary, then we prevent damage. This will be possible sometimes, but of course not all the time.

    There are many things we can reduce, from power and fuel, to raw materials and excess equipment. Every time we reduce, we avoid creating unnecessary damage, and are usually reducing costs at the same time.

2) **Reuse.** If an attacker does try to use force against a martial artist, they will often (depending on the martial art being practiced)redirect the energy of the attack, while minimizing harm to either party.

   This then becomes the guideline to our second line of defense. If we do indeed need to engage,we should look for a way to use what already exists.

   Reusing minimizes the amount of embodied energy and raw materials used for a given number of tasks. For example, avoid using disposable cups at the water cooler. Over the lifetime of a reusable cup, less material and energy is required than if a new cup is used every time someone wants a drink.

   There are some more advanced strategies for reusing too. These we will discuss in a later chapter.

3) **Recycle.** If the situation has become difficult to manage and harm cannot be avoided, then the martial artist will interject some of their power to turn an attacking move to their advantage. This is only done when the previous two approaches are not possible.

   Therefore, recycling becomes the RLS eco-warrior's last line of defense, not his first. Recycling still causes harm. It may do less damage than not recycling, but it still requires energy, and in the case of plastics especially, can produce unwanted toxins.

The RLS is always looking to find solutions that minimize harm to others and the planet. Their objective is to leave the world a better place while providing value to customers and financially taking care of themselves and their employees.

To fully achieve this, it is important to understand that reducing negative impact is not the same as reversing it. Reducing harm is a step in the right direction, but in today's world,it goes nowhere near far enough.

The next rule has been around for at least a couple thousand years: do unto others as you would have done unto yourself (or words to this effect).This is so important that it is often referred to as the "Golden Rule," and is found in religions and cultures around the world.

So how does it apply to businesses?

I would suggest it means we need to look after other people properly. That is, we should ensure everyone is paid fairly, that people are not taken advantage of, that we guarantee their health and safety, and that we don't deplete their resources or pollute their food, water, or air. You may think this is basic common sense. Yet this is far from common; in fact, it is extremely rare.

Which leads us to the next rule, take responsibility.

RLSs must assume full responsibility for cleaning up their share of the mess they create. We are taught this principle as children but somehow forget it as adults.

The way many businesses operate is to go around raping and pillaging the planet, taking the profits, and running. They then expect taxpayers' money and charities to run around cleaning up their mess. While I am sure this does not include you, I can almost guarantee it does include companies you do business with (either directly or indirectly).

It is with this in mind that the Real-Life Superhero adds a fourth R rule to live by...

4) **Restore.** If we do have to create unavoidable damage as a business, it is surely our responsibility to restore it back to its original state as much as possible.

    If it were the law that companies needed to clean up their mess, you can be sure they would become much better at the reducing, reusing, and recycling!

In the coming chapters, we will look at how we can apply these guidelines in a more practical way. However, should you find a situation where the following strategies are insufficient or ineffective, use the guidelines as a foundation to design more targeted solutions for your specific needs.

REAL-LIFE SUPERHERO PROFILE

Business Name: Dental Healing

Business Type: Dentist

Founded By: Dr. Chester Yokoyama

Year Established: 1997

Mission: To deliver holistic dental care while ensuring minimal negative impact on the environment.

Powers: Reduce dental pain and suffering in the community, reduce power usage, conserve water, educate customers, and use low-impact materials where possible.

The Story: A dental clinic may not be the obvious place to start for superhero sustainability. But that is the point. We need sustainability superheroes in every industry.

Dr. Yokoyama understood the dental needs of clients, but he also understood the responsibility as a business owner to minimize his environmental impact. As a business owner, he also saw the financial benefits from doing the right thing.

He set about transforming his clinic by giving it an energy and water conservation overhaul. This included new HVAC ducting, ENERGY STAR certified equipment, a new highly efficient on-demand air compressor, Water Sense certified plumbing, a waterless vacuum, and a paperless filing system.

These changes created an estimated 35 percent reduction in operating costs and will pay for themselves in just three to five years.

In alignment with the low-impact philosophy, the clinic made use of repurposed furniture and eco-friendly materials, such as bamboo flooring.

In addition to this Dr. Yokoyama made sure that all paint, adhesives, glues, and sealants, etc., used were VOC free, which is better for the environment, his staff, and his customers. They also only use Green Seal certified cleaning supplies.

Not only have these changes reduced operating costs, but they have helped him get media attention too, including a feature in The Huffington Post. The focus on sustainability provides him with a marketing edge over the local competition and provides an example to other businesses of what can be achieved.

Dental Healing became the first dental practice in Los Angeles to be certified as a green business, and has been recognized as a climate leader by the State of California.

Websites: www.dentalhealing.com

A CONFLICT OF INTEREST

> **"I'm sure they have good reason."**
> —Natasha Romanova (The Black Widow)

In 1924 two things happened that would act as catalysts to increase consumerism and consequently an accelerated consumption of raw materials and energy. The first came under the guidance of Alfred P. Sloan Jr. when General Motors began to create an annual design update to their cars. This change was designed to create the desire in car owners to replace their cars on a more frequent basis, thereby driving sales (forgive the pun).

The second was considerably more sinister . . .

On December 23 of the same year, a group of light bulb manufacturers, including the likes of OSRAM, Phillips, and General Electric, formed the rather ominous sounding "Phoebus Cartel."[46] Its purpose? To deliberately limit the lifespan of electric light bulbs. Why?

Well, the longest lasting light bulb known can be found in a fire station in Livermore, USA. It has been running almost nonstop for over 115 years. If they made bulbs like they used to, you would probably never need replace them during your lifetime. That is great for the environment and for your wallet, but not so good for companies selling them.

The Phoebus Cartel set a limit of 1,000 hours of life for every bulb. If any manufacturer was caught selling bulbs that exceeded this limit, they would be fined severely by the group. Over the years these ideas from GM and the Phoebus Cartel caught on with many other businesses and became known as planned obsolescence.

We now see a variety of strategies for increasing this type of repeat business.

- **Contrived durability** reduces the life expectancy of a product by designing it to wear out quicker than necessary, either through lower quality manufacturing or weaker materials.

- **Prevention of repairs** is a strategy that tries to prevent owners from fixing items once a fault does occur (think Apple products).

- **Style obsolescence** tries to get consumers to buy by continuously creating new designs and positioning old models as out of date (think the fashion industry, and of course iPhones).

- **Systemic obsolescence** prevents the compatibility of new and old systems. You often find this in software, or some hardware designs, forcing consumers to upgrade periodically.

- **Programmed obsolescence** is perhaps the most unnecessary and evil of them all. This is when manufacturers deliberately program something to break even when there is nothing wrong with it. The most famous example of this is with ink jet printers. Many manufacturers began adding a chip to disable the printer after a fixed number of uses, or shortly after the guarantee expired. (No, it was not your imagination.)

While great for economic growth, planned obsolescence is nothing short of disgraceful from a sustainability perspective. It is also one of the biggest conflicts of interest for any Real-Life Superhero business owner. Thankfully we are starting to see a return of companies making products that last. Ironically, one of the best examples of this comes back full circle to the American car industry. Tesla has done away with the yearly design updates, instead making continual gradual

improvements, with many of the changes coming as software updates for existing owners.

Clothing companies such as Patagonia and Kathmandu also now have active policies to design clothes to last longer so customers will not need to replace them as often. And the good news, neither of them have gone out of business! In a world where products are designed to fail, having ones that are designed to last may once again be a good business strategy.

There is undoubtedly an economic argument for planned obsolescence, but certainly not an environmental one—hence the potential conflict of interest (that is, if you are not a Real-Life Superhero). For the RLS there is no question. The people and planet come first.

Instead of opting for the easy route to profit, an RLS becomes more creative and intelligent in their business strategy. In doing so, they can win the minds and hearts of customers and take us that one step closer to forging business and environmental landscapes that can coexist without conflict.

CLOSE THE LOOP

"One man's trash is another man's treasure, and the by-product
from one food can be perfect for making another."
—Yotam Ottolenghi

One of the keys to creating genuine sustainability is to create closed loop systems. Indeed, this is the very concept behind the sustainability and recycle logos (the triangle in the form of a never-ending Möbius loop). In many ways, the very core principle of reuse and recycle can be summarized by this idea that one man's trash is another man's treasure.

To do business with our previously designed guidelines, we need to reduce waste. The closed loop system does this in a way that minimizes energy loss by repurposing waste of one system for use in another. (i.e. Reusing and recycling.)

Let's look at a simple example: food waste. Many businesses produce food waste in a variety of forms. Much of this currently ends up in a landfill, which is wastage that borders on the criminally insane.

Waste food can easily be used to feed other people or animals, or turned into compost to grow more food. It just depends on the type, quantity, and quality of the food that is thrown away.

Excess heat, waste water, scrap wood or metal, manure, and many other things that are often considered waste can be used either by the same business that created the initial waste or by another.

Some companies take waste cooking oil and turn it into biodiesel, others take plastic bags and use them to make building bricks, and some take scrap paper and repurpose it into notebooks. The list is endless.

Many businesses have multiple opportunities for reusing their own waste. A senior engineer for the Shangri-La Hotel in Chiang Mai explained to me how they were recycling the water from the air-conditioning units, something I had never even considered!

When you think about it, most air-conditioning systems have two unintentional outputs, water and heat. Both of these are useful, and yet almost every air-conditioner just disposes of them as waste.

A coal powered chemical plant in India has started to collect their CO_2 emissions (thanks to technology provided by Carbon Clean Solutions), which can then be turned into a range of products, including baking powder, glass, sweeteners and detergents.[47] This commercialization allows for the carbon capture to run without subsidy, providing an additional revenue stream for the factory. Good environmentalism can make good business sense.

Closing the loops to better manage waste is something that will require individual approaches in every business. Take the time to give your own business an audit. Look around your office, in your bins, your drains, and remember to involve your team. Explain the concept and get everyone looking for wastage throughout the business.

Document it all, and then find ways to either reduce the waste, reuse or repurpose it internally, or recycle it by finding other businesses that will see it not as waste, but as a resource. Again, get everyone involved in coming up with suggestions to each of your different types of unused output. Collective intelligence can often come up with some surprising solutions.

As Doctor Octopus instructs, "Intelligence is not a privilege, it's a gift. And you use it for the good of mankind."[48] When we put our minds to it, we can close the loops, reduce wastage, reduce energy loss, and increase overall efficiency. Closing loops will almost always lead to both cost savings and a more environmentally sustainable business. This is not only a reflection of intelligence, but is also good for all mankind.

AN EFFICIENT SYSTEM

> "Efficiency is doing better what is already being done."
> —Peter Drucker

System efficiency sounds like it has more of a place on the factory floor than it does in environmental protection. Yet it is our ability to create more efficient systems that enable us to reduce wasted energy, raw materials, and pollution. System efficiency also improves profit margins and increases our ability to scale our business. And this is true for just about every type of business you can think of, from pudding factories and plumbers to independent consultants and comic book illustrators.

We have already talked about closing the loop, which is one very particular and important part of system efficiency. But we need to dive much deeper into the rabbit hole than that.

We can think of any business as being a system. Each system fits into a much larger system called society. It is also made up of many smaller systems (such as accounting, stock control, sales, etc., each of which is made of subsystems). In addition to these systems, your business links to many other complex systems, known as other businesses.

Every system needs energy to operate, and each has a required input and an expected output. The more efficient the system, the less energy (time, money, raw materials, electricity,etc.) we need to put in to get the same level of output. For example, let's say our goal was to produce one hundred cherry pies.

Making each one individually and baking them one at a time is very inefficient. It will take much longer, use more manpower, and require

more energy for the oven. Making a large quantity of mix and baking them together in a larger single oven is a much more efficient system.

The need for efficiency may seem obvious,but it never ceases to amaze me how much inefficiency creeps into businesses overtime. These inefficiencies show up in many forms, big and small. Take something as simple as responding to your superhero communications network(also known as checking your e-mail).

I have seen a lot of inboxes, and I would say less than 1 percent are managed well. If your inbox is like most, it is filled with hundreds, possibly thousands, of e-mails. These stretch back weeks, months, or even years. Important messages are quickly forgotten, and looking through to try to find one from even the past few days can be time-consuming.

Having to deal with my fair share of e-mail, I looked for a more efficient solution. Now I have a simple process that I follow whenever I check my inbox:

1) Scan through any that are bulk or junk mail. If I have found my way onto someone's e-mail list, I unsubscribe and then delete it. If some spam has slipped through my spam filter, I just delete them without even opening (or as soon as I realize it is spam).

2) If an e-mail is something I will expect regularly but I don't need to read it, then I set a rule to auto-archive any future e-mail that is the same. These are mostly bank statements or utility bills (that are all set to auto pay). This way I never need to see them again (unless I want to).

3) Each of the remaining e-mails, I open and process immediately. First, if possible, I try to delegate it. This is easy, just forward to the right person with a short one-line explanation if needed. If I must personally respond and I can do so quickly, then I write a quick reply and archive the e-mail. If the e-mail requires some time to process and I don't have time, then it stays in the inbox until I do.

I call this my zero-inbox policy, as my goal is to keep my inbox as empty as humanly possible. The result? After I have checked my inbox, I rarely have more than two or three e-mails at any one time. More often than not, it will be empty. This process has several main advantages:

1) I am not overwhelmed by my inbox. Inbox overwhelm is very common, and it can lead to procrastination and stress. And procrastinating is about the most inefficient thing you can do!

2) If someone has sent me a message, they get a response quickly. This means the sender is not left waiting, which can have a knock-on effect causing unnecessary delays.

3) Important e-mails are not forgotten or lost under a pile of junk messages.

4) When I open my inbox, I can clearly see what I need to do. Any remaining e-mails act as a to-do list.

5) Time spent managing e-mail is greatly reduced. This reduces my computer's energy usage. Good for my productivity and for the environment.

6) By removing myself from most lists, and by auto-archiving bills, etc., I reduce the carbon footprint of my inbox. (More on this later.)

From a business perspective, these benefits are obvious. But why, apart from the reduced e-mail carbon footprint, is this also better for the environment?

It all comes down to the compound effect and hidden costs of inefficiency. The longer someone is checking their e-mail, the more lighting and air-conditioning they will need. The more time others spend chasing them up on forgotten or delayed responses, the more energy those people will be using. For every day a person spends in the office, a commute is needed. The footprint of every task anyone does must calculate its share of this commute.

To keep it simple, assume Sally's commute to work generated 8kgs of CO_2. If she works eight hours per day and spends one hour on e-mail, then the act of checking e-mail creates an additional 1kg of CO_2 (on top of the existing e-mail footprint). If she reduces this time to thirty minutes, then the environmental impact of that specific task (i.e., checking e-mail) is reduced by 0.5kgs every day. The financial cost of getting this task completed (i.e., her salary) will be halved also.

This may not sound like a huge amount, but given that the average person works approximately 260 days of the year, that would add up to 130kgs. Over ten years it would equal 1,300kgs of CO_2, and with ten employees there would be a savings of 13,000kgs of CO_2 (over the ten years). All from making the process of checking e-mail more efficient.

This concept applies to all tasks. Employees, and even many business owners, think of economic and environmental footprints in terms of fixed quantities. An employee's travel is 8kg/day, so 40kg/week. The employee earns $200/day, so $1,000/per week. But this is really a bad way to calculate the costs on either level. It's better instead to think about input versus output.

Each system in your business has an input and an output, as does each task within that system. By increasing the efficiency of those systems and their associated tasks, you reduce costs and your environmental footprint. You also increase speed, allowing your business to scale faster or to simply get the same output in less time and with less cost.

This principle applies to almost everything, even your lighting. Each light has an input and an output. Not all lights are created equal, with some producing the same amount of light (lumens) with far less energy (watts). We will look at this in more detail, along with a variety of other ways to reduce other specific inefficiencies, in the next section. What is paramount though is not the specific recommendations, but the principles that underlie them. Once you understand these, you can look for opportunities throughout your business to make improvements.

THE BIG 3

Let's get down to bare basics for one minute. We need to fasten our capes and fly up high to see the big picture.

Imagine flying over the world and looking down on cities, towns, villages, and millions of isolated homes. You see the people going about their lives, and you notice that no matter who they are or where in the world they live, they all need three critical things: air, water, and food.

These three things are essential for life and define our ability to be healthy. If we think about poisons in our environment, no matter if from power generation, transport, agriculture, building materials, packaging, electronics, or the production of textiles, the way they affect us comes down to the degree to which they pollute or harm the quality of our air, water, or food.

As a Real-Life Superhero, we need to evaluate the impact of our business on these big three. Start by examining your own business directly, and then work back and look at your supply chain and your service providers. Just spend a couple of minutes following the chain back in your mind. Who supplies your suppliers, what equipment do they use, how many companies are involved in each computer, tool, piece of machinery, service,etc. required to make that equipment, and so on?

With each step consider what raw materials are needed? What damage is done to the land? What pollution is dumped into the air or water? What energy is used, and how is it produced?

This is a great exercise, as it helps you fully appreciate how interconnected businesses are and the hidden damage that occurs as a result of us doing business (or being a consumer). So let's take a better look at each of these essential three components to life, and why we should care.

AIR

We can live for days without water, weeks without food, but just minutes without air. And yet we rarely give air much of a thought, nor do we treat it with much respect or consideration.

The closest we think about air is usually regarding greenhouse gases. And, yes, we have a big problem with CO_2, methane, and other GHGs (greenhouse gases). While they may get plenty of attention in the media, they are far from the only issue.

There are many harmful particles and poisonous gases that are released into the air from energy production, transportation, pesticides, burning of forests or fields, and of course the air pollution from factories.

Approximately 5.5 million people die every year from air pollution. The worst hit areas are not surprisingly in China and India, but many more are sick and dying in developed countries.

The European Environment Agency has calculated that in Europe alone air pollution annually costs anything from 59 to 189 billion euros.[49] And this is just the economic cost. It does not take into account the physical or emotional pain and suffering of those affected, or their families. This amounts to millions of people and billions of dollars, within an area which has some of the strictest antipollution policies in the world.

Another contributor to air pollution is our dependency on plastic. The extraction of oil and natural gas used to make plastic, along with its manufacturing process, produces a range of different toxic chemicals into the air. These include benzene, toluene, ethyl benzene, carbon monoxide, hydrogen sulfide, sulfur dioxide, formaldehyde, and a range of dioxins.

Some plastics also outgas for months after they have been manufactured. This outgassing (sometimes called off gassing) can lead to phthalate contamination in our homes, which is linked to a range of endocrine-related illnesses.

Assuming we then recycle plastic, it needs to be heated, a process that releases more toxic gases. (Remember, recycling is NOT environmentally friendly. It is usually, though not always, just less damaging than not recycling.)

And that's just plastic. "Safe" levels of air pollution are calculated by looking at the type and amount of pollution when produced in isolation. They do not consider the effects of combining different types of pollution that may be in the same environment, or of accumulating pollution levels. If we had only one product or business that created air pollution, it would likely be insignificant, but with so many the problems are only escalating.

Another unwanted side effect of air pollution is its knock-on effects through water. Acid rain (caused primarily by sulfur and nitrogen oxides in the air) is damaging not just our buildings but our lakes, forests, and many crops too. Meanwhile, the world's oceans are becoming increasingly acidic due to rising levels of CO_2, which is having a devastating effect on marine life.

Governments are simply not doing enough. We need Real-Life Superheroes to step up and create products or services that help address these issues. And we need companies who currently use the existing solutions (e.g.,oil-based plastic) to switch and start using the alternative options (e.g., glass).

As Leonardo DiCaprio explained at a United Nations award ceremony, "To those who may be discouraged by naysayers, let me remind you, the environmental awakening is all over the world and the progress we have made so far . . . has always been because of people, not governments." [50]

COMMON AIR POLLUTANTS, THEIR SOURCES AND PATHOLOGICAL EFFECTS ON HUMAN BODY

Pollutants	Sources	Pathological Effect on Human Body
Aldehydes	Thermal decomposition of fats, oil or glycerol.	Irritate nasal and respiratory tract.
Ammonia	Chemical process-dye making, explosives, fertilizers	Inflame upper respiratory passages.
Arsenic	Processes involving metal or acids containing arsenic soldering.	Break down the red cell in blood jaundice.
Carbon monoxide	Gasoline motor exhausts, burning of coal.	Reduce O_2 carrying capacity of blood.
Chlorine	Bleaching cotton and Hour: man other chemical processes.	Attack entire respiratory tract and mucous membrane of eyes, cause pulmonary edema.
Hydrogen cyanides	Fumigation blast furnaces, metal plating.	Interfere with nerve cells, produce dry throat, indistinct vision, headache.
Hydrogen fluorides	Petroleum rating, glass etching, Al, and fertilizers production.	Irritate and corrode all body passages.
Hydrogen sulphides	Refineries and chemical industries bituminous fuels.	Smell like rotten eggs, cause nausea, irritate eyes and throat.
Nitrogen oxides	Motor vehicles exhaust soft coal.	Inhibit ciliary action of the nose so that soot and dust penetrate far into the lungs.
Phosgenes (carbonyl chloride ($COCl_2$)	Chemical and dye manufacturing.	Induce coughing, irritation, and sometimes fatal pulmonary edema.
Sulphur	Coal and oil combustion Incineratory.	Causes chest constriction, headache, vomiting, and death from respiratory ailments.
Suspended particles (ash, soot, smoke)	Incinerator, almost any type of manufacturing.	Cause emphysema, eye irritation and possibly cancer.

51

You can be one of those people. It is within your power to further progress, and help protect the innocent from being harmed by the very air they have no choice but to breathe.

WATER

Water is the most miraculous substance known to man. It is the essence of life itself, has many unique and unexplained properties, covers approximately 71 percent of the planet, and makes up about 60 percent of our bodies. Even so, we treat it with almost total disregard.

I am aware there are some regulations in place, and sadly the situation would certainly be much worse if we didn't. But these laws do not come close to protecting us from ourselves.

The world's water can be broken down into two general categories: fresh water and salt water. Freshwater is, of course, essential for drinking, farming, and keeping all other land-based plants and animals alive.

Salt water, on the other hand, is home to countless species, some of which we also use for food. However, it is one group of the smallest species, phytoplankton, that is essential to our survival. Phytoplankton are forms of tiny plant life which are responsible for producing 50–85 percent of all oxygen on earth[52] (and help absorb 30–50 percent of the world's CO_2).

Many businesses are apparently run by people who have not yet figured out these basics or who continue to turn a blind eye to the damage they are indirectly doing. Maybe the decreasing oxygen levels are starting to decrease our intelligence levels!

If you are shipping products around the world, your business depends on transportation that is damaging the oceans. If you sell or rely on meat or dairy, your business is almost certainly causing harm to fresh water ways and oceans. If your business uses textiles or paper, chances are it too is helping perpetuate the degradation of the earth's water. Use leather, plastics, or electronics? Yup, you guessed it . . .

The planet's oceans contain five major gyres. These are giant naturally occurring vortices of water that are hundreds of kilometres wide. In recent years, they have been gaining attention,as they are turning into giant garbage dumps.

How bad have things become?

In a recent study of the North Atlantic Gyre, it was found that plastic now outnumbers phytoplankton (remember, that stuff we need to survive), by 46:1.[54] And here's the truly scary part: we produced more plastic in the first ten years of this century than we did in all of history before 2,000. And we are continuing to produce more at an alarming rate.

This plastic build-up is affecting wildlife too. Birds, fish, turtles, whales, and dolphins are directly affected, with many losing their life every year to this pollution. At least 100,000 marine animals and over 1,000,000 birds lose their life to plastic every year.[55] The full extent of the damage is still unknown.

As business owners, we need to realize that while we may have no control over how our packaging gets disposed, we do have control over what needs to be disposed of in the first place.

It is not just the floating trash we can see that is a problem though. There is also a huge amount of heavy metals and other toxins which are poisoning the very water we depend on for our survival. Many of these metals and toxins start their life as wastewater that is dumped into rivers, or they leach through the ground and find their way into freshwater systems, before eventually finding their way into our oceans.

Once in the water, they start building up in the smaller marine life, before being consumed by bigger creatures. This process continues up the food chain with the largest species containing dangerously high levels of heavy metals, which in our infinite wisdom,we then eat.

Common culprits include lead, mercury, chromium, and cadmium. These can cause a host of different health and environmental issues and are the result of numerous industrial processes.

Try to visualize it for a moment. You can almost see the comic book villain laughing hysterically as he watches the toxic green spill heading toward the city reservoir. Then, just at the last minute the superhero swoops in and saves the day.

Right now, are you the villain or the hero? A tough question to face,as most of us won't like the answer. While we may not be standing and gloating as the toxic spill flows toward unsuspecting citizens, most businesses are contributing toward a scenario all too similar. It may be harder to see and be slower acting, but it is real,and it is dangerous nonetheless. Out of sight and out of mind, but not out of body.

If this is making you a little uncomfortable, then good. Embrace the feeling. Change often begins when the pain of remaining where we are becomes greater than the pain of moving.

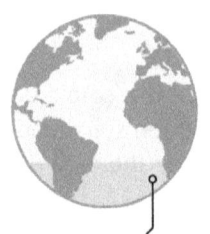

Only **2.5%** of the earths water is **fresh water** [56]

70% of water used is for **agriculture**[57]

40,000 to **110,000** metric tons of trash is thrown into the ocean by **American**s per year.[59]

Plastic in the oceans and coastal areas kill **100,000+ marine mammals,** over **1 million** birds, and **countless fish**[58]

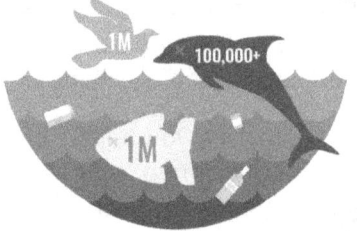

Polluted water kills **4,500 children** per day[60]

In the **North Atlantic Gyre** plastic outnumbers plankton **46·1**.[61]

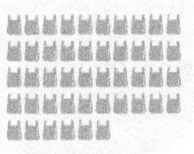

In the **US**, **40% of rivers** and **46% of lakes** are too polluted for swimming, fishing or marine life.[62]

A single drop of used motor oil can contaminate **1 million drops** of water.[63]

FOOD

The English eat to live. The French live to eat. Regardless of which way you look at it, food is fundamental to life. How, then, have we allowed our food to decline to such a sorry state?

Food has become increasingly artificial, much of it unrecognis able compared to food just a few decades ago. Increased processing and refinement, the addition of artificial ingredients, and even modification at the genetic level have meant that our diets have become severely distorted, and we have an entirely new sense of what is "normal."

Even our fruits and vegetables now suffer from the addition of a host of artificial fertilizers and pesticides due to intensive farming methods and the influence of big agrochemical companies. A recent study by Dr Liam Goucher, found that approximately 43 percent of the carbon footprint from a loaf of bread came from the fertilizers used to grow the wheat.[64] Then there are the additional toxins from transport, industry, and mining that find their way into our food through the pollution of the air, water, and land.

Let's not forget meat and dairy. Ignore for a moment the impact they have on our water and air;they themselves have become laden with chemicals, antibiotics, and hormones.

Essentially we have all become part of the largest experiment ever conducted on how much toxicity the human body can tolerate. Rather worryingly, the early data is not looking good. While we have not wiped ourselves out as a species (yet), we are killing off huge numbers, and many more of us are becoming very sick.

In 2012, UN Secretary-General Ban Ki-moon warned everyone that, "Commercial overexploitation of the world's fish stocks is severe, many species have been hunted to fractions of their original populations. More than half of global fisheries are exhausted, and a further third are depleted."[65]

The sad part is that much of this loss comes from by catch. That is, the fish and other marine life that are caught unintentionally while catching target species. In the case of shrimping, as much as 80 percent of the entire catch is thrown back for dead. The defense for this senseless killing? Economics. This way of doing business is mindless short-term thinking on every level. Once the fish have gone, so will the fishing industry's income and much of the world's food supply—not to mention the loss of biodiversity.

Talking of shrimp, approximately 25 percent of the world's shrimp comes from Thailand. Many of the Thai shrimping boats are manned by illegal immigrant slaves that are held in captivity, beaten, worked eighteen-hour days on a bowl of rice, and thrown overboard to die if they become too weak to work. In the twenty-first century, it is shocking to learn this type of behavior continues, but so long as we keep supporting it financially, I guess it should not come as such a great surprise.

Most people fail to realize how close to collapse our marine ecosystems are. According to scientists from Dalhousie University, between 1950 and 2000numbers of large predator fish declined by 90 percent,and their numbers continue to decline.[66] This devastation has been driven almost entirely as a result of business doing what it does.

Some would claim that business has only been trying to meet demand. However, I would argue that it is business that has created much of this demand. Through a combination of reducing the cost of fish through industrial fishing practices and marketing to increase consumer desire, demand is much higher now than it once was. Population growth only magnifies (not causes) this problem.

These issues within our food supply have not been caused by any single individual or business. Instead,they are the net result of two simple things: not knowing better, and putting profit before people. We can no longer claim the former, which now only leaves the latter.

But what about the jobs? What about people's right to eat fish? Well, as fish stocks decline it will become increasing unviable to continue commercial fishing, until eventually a tipping point will be reached. Once this happens, both the jobs and the choice to eat fish will be gone anyway.

While on the topic of food, it may be more suited to feed Frankenstein than humans, but as a reader of this book, your food is at least likely to be abundant. Given the rising obesity levels (and the associated health issues), some would argue too abundant. For nearly 2 billion other people though, food remains scarce. One in four people are undernourished, causing 3.1 million children to die every year from either starvation or illnesses related to malnutrition.[67] (an average of almost one death every ten seconds).

Sadly, much of this malnutrition comes down to one single cause: poverty. You only need to look at the multitude of desert towns, and even the international space station, to see that remote locations or harsh conditions are no reason to go without food. You just need sufficient money.

Unfortunately, all too often the reason these poverty-stricken regions are so poor is that most companies that operate in these areas take as much as they can while paying as little as they can and giving as little as possible back to the communities they exploit.

These industries include mining, manufacturing, and farming. In other words, the very fabric of virtually every business.

This way of doing business sounds like the work of a master evil villain again. I don't know of any superhero that would allow or partake in this type of injustice. Yes, my friend, the challenges ahead can feel overwhelming. But you are not alone, and together we have the power to create change.

In the **US**, **31%** of its 2010 food supply went uneaten[68]

Estimated **168 liters** of water required to make **1 pint** of beer.[69]

Approx **15,400 liters** of water required to produce **1kg** of beef.[40]

39.2kg of CO_2 generated for every **1kg** of lamb produced[70]

Approximately **50%** of the carbon footprint of a loaf of bread comes from the fertilizers used to grow the wheat.[71]

Over **50 chemicals** used to make strawberry flavor in a fast food milkshake.[72]

94% of all soy crops in the **US** are now genetically modified.[73]

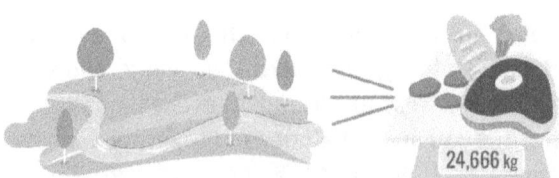

1 acre of land can produce either **24,666 kg** of plant-based foods, or just **113kg** of meat.73 (That's about 218x the amount.)[74]

THE SINGULARITY

No, not the artificial intelligence singularity that may eliminate us all and make this book irrelevant in fractions of a second. I am talking about the singular point that unifies the big three we have just examined (and indeed, this entire book). The singularity that I am referring to is us. That is, humanity.

While I interviewed Oliver Millner, the sustainability coordinator for the Kathmandu clothing brand, he explained to me that they have one guiding principle: people.

When you figure out what is good for people, then everything else will fall into place. That does not mean we should pay everyone crazy high salaries so they can live in big houses, drive big cars, and take big holidays. That may be what a lot of people want, but it is not what is always best for us as a whole (and often not them individually either).

Fair salaries, good air, good water, good food, and a healthy natural environment is what people really need, and ultimately this is what is best for the planet too. It is only when people start trying to take more than their share, get greedy, and start damaging the world in the process,that the problems begin.

For a long time, capitalists have claimed that it is the free economy that drives innovation. And while this may be true for some, I would not agree that it is true for most.

Many scientists, inventors, artists, and even entrepreneurs have created and strived for improvement. Not for money, fame, or fortune, but because of their passion. Money helps make the world go around and may fund technological innovation, but it is far from the driving force. That driving force is the creative human spirit. Unfortunately, many people have lost sight of this, which perhaps in part explains why the developed world is on so many anti depressants and why there are so many therapies centered around reconnecting to creativity.

When we put people's wellbeing first, not people's greed, then both society and the planet will benefit.

On a side note, I should clarify. While I may criticize the way capitalism is being practiced, I am not supporting communism or socialism. There is a tendency to jump to conclusions that if you are not "this," then you must be "that." I am not supporting any specific ideology, other than putting society's wellbeing before individual or corporate greed.

I am not against making a profit. I am, however, against making a profit if it means that someone is paid just one or two dollars per day to work twelve to sixteen hours so we can buy a tee-shirt for a few cents less while the companies manufacturing and selling those tee-shirts make excessive profits. Companies such as Kathmandu and Patagonia are showing this approach is just not necessary.

We need to find ways to continue progress and live comfortable lives, but in ways that do not compromise humanity or the health of the planet. I believe we now have much of the technology to achieve this, and we certainly have the intelligence to figure any remaining solutions we may need. The question is, will we work together globally and stop putting individual short-term interests first?

And this, my budding RLS, is your biggest challenge: to apply this principle of putting people first throughout all areas of your business, and to help educate and encourage others to do the same.

REAL-LIFE SUPERHERO PROFILE

Business Name: The Natural Paint Company

Business Type: Paint and varnish

Founded By: James Mount and Grace Glass

Year Established: 2015

Mission: To make a social and environmental difference by reducing the production and use of toxic chemicals in the paint industry, and to make healthier living environments the first choice.

Powers: Reduce the production and use of toxic chemicals, make our work and living environments safer, produce products that are naturally recycled by nature (rather than leaving a toxic footprint), and create greater consumer awareness of the dangers and problems associated with traditional paints.

The Story: Based in the South Island of New Zealand, James and Grace decided to build a business that would make a social and environmental difference.

Together they shared a vision to reduce the production and use of toxic chemicals in the paint industry. This became the beginning of an incredible journey to develop the first natural paints created in New Zealand, for New Zealand conditions.

Both still in their early twenties, they had to use their limited savings, borrow money from family, and take a bank loan to kick start their business.

James was motivated by the desire to build his own business while making a social and environmental difference. Grace, then working as a nurse, loved the fact they were building a company that helped prevent sickness, rather than having to try and cure it.

To achieve their vision, they decided to use ingredients with the following qualities:

- Can be found in nature

- Come from self-renewing resources

- Can be safely recycled by nature after use

- Have minimal impact on the environment and their employees during manufacturing

The more they learned about the industry, the more determined they were to succeed. While offering a step in the right direction, many existing paints that carry Eco label certifications and "No VOCs" labels are still laden with toxic ingredients.

They designed their products to contain natural insecticides and pesticides, which repel insects and inhibit the growth of mold without the need for dangerous chemicals. This has the additional benefit that they significantly reduce the amount of toxins released into the air during and after painting. This means freshly painted rooms smell great (rather than of overpowering poisonous fumes).

Indeed, not only were they able to make a product that matched market standards, but much of their range actually exceeded the quality of their competition.

Despite being such a young business they already have a significant range of products, and many happy customers. They have experienced exponential growth in a very short time, and Grace has now quite her job to work fulltime on the business.

As with the other Real-Life Superheroes featured in this book, James and Grace's products are able to successfully compete in a highly competitive market; not despite their focus on sustainability, but because of it. They provide a shining example that doing the right thing can give you not just a better product, but also a huge marketing advantage.

Websites: www.naturalpaint.co.nz

YOU HAVE THE POWER, NOW USE IT

> "At any given moment, you have the power to say:
> this is not how the story is going to end."
>
> —Christine Mason Miller

Study after study has shown if you feel powerless, you are more likely just to give up. You must remember, you do have power, and you can create change. In fact, as a business owner, you have more power to create change than most.

As we have pointed out, consumers cause little environmental damage—other than through the consumption and use of the products and services they buy. When Tim drives to work and burns petrol to get there, it is the product he is consuming that causes the problem. When Mandy buys her new shoes, it is not the act of buying or wearing the shoes that causes damage, it is the raw materials and production of those oh so uncomfortable and bad for your back "but they're sparkly and make me look taller" heels.

John would no doubt prefer it if he knew that his drive to work was not damaging the planet. But he needs to get to work. Mandy is unlikely to take any delight in the knowledge of the human suffering and misery that made her new heels possible. But they were on special!

When you think about it, much of the actual damage done is by the large mining, power, petroleum, and agrochemical corporations. Either directly through their operations or indirectly through the use of their products (such as burning petrol).

But their customers are the small to medium businesses. Few of these big corporations sell directly to the average Joe. Their products are sold to other business who either use their products to create new products or resell to the end consumer. (While branded, even the big gas stations are just franchises.)

Their power is in their money. And their money comes from you. Yes, even you and I are financing Dr. Evil.

What's more, they know this, which is why they are afraid of anything that threatens their domination. These corporations spend megabucks trying to prevent you from having access to alternatives. Is it any wonder then that it was the same think tanks and "scientists" that were hired by big tobacco to convince us smoking was safe, that are now being hired by petrochemical companies to convince us climate change is a joke?

Even a small amount of research into the lineup of dubious characters behind these organizations will trigger some serious alarm bells. (For more information on this I highly recommend reading Merchants of Doubt or watching the documentary of the same name, which is based on the book.)

The truth is, they need you more than you need them. Maybe not you individually, but us collectively.

Here lies the catch 22. The average business still needs to use fuel, electricity, and products made of plastic or other non-renewable raw materials, or relies on doing business with other small- to medium-sized businesses that are using these products. How then can we escape this vicious cycle?

If we simply gave up using anything that may have an adverse social or environmental impact, or indirectly fund these mega corporations, then our businesses would collapse in days. If this happened, then we would lose our incomes and ironically, most of our power to create or influence meaningful change.

On the other hand, if we do nothing, then we will continue to strengthen the enemy and be a part of the problem. There must be another option. If not, we are almost certainly doomed.

A brief side note: If you think potential Armageddon is a melodramatic exaggeration, then think again. Several mathematicians and scientists have calculated that our chances of being wiped out by the end of the century are disturbingly high.

Dr. Simpson, a mathematician at the University of Barcelona, has calculated there is a 0.2 percent likelihood humanity could be extinct in the year, or a 13 percent likelihood by the end of the century. (This is significantly more optimistic than Sir Martin Rees, a British astronomer who put our odds of making it to 2100 at only 50 percent.)[75]

Regardless of the precise accuracy of these numbers, there is certainly some statistical probability of annihilation. It is easy to become very depressed by this news. Many people lean toward taking a fatalistic perspective, which only increases these doomsday odds.

A much healthier attitude is to be positive, yet proactive. Turned around, Dr. Simpson is also saying we have a 99.8 percent chance of surviving the year and an 87 percent chance of making the end of the century. And, by any degree of rational thought, we should be working to improve these more optimistic odds (whatever the actual number), not reduce them.

So back to our catch 22, how do we deal with this dependency on large corporations whose way of doing business is putting the planet's future in jeopardy?

The answer lies in a multi-pronged approach. Use your power to:

Reduce our consumption as much as possible (through avoiding buying more than we need and increasing overall efficiency). The less we buy, the less profit they make and the less power they have, and the less damage there is done to the environment.

Switch to B2B providers who have genuine active sustainability programs in place. While no business can call itself truly green, supporting those who are making ongoing efforts to reduce their impact is important.

Make the change to renewable energy and clean transport systems as soon as is practical.

Be vocal online and offline regarding your disapproval to the current system. Having an opinion is worthless if we don't act on that view or make it known. Both companies and governments respond to large-scale public opinion (eventually). If they feel their position of power is being threatened, then most will adapt and change their position to survive. (Over time those that don't will become obsolete.)

Actively create businesses that provide better solutions. Again, Tesla has provided an excellent example of this by introducing better alternatives to gas-powered cars, as well as methods to generate and store renewable energy in your home. While there are an increasing number of such examples, we still have many more challenges to solve that will require an army of smart and proactive entrepreneurs.

As entrepreneurs and business owners, we create and supply the products and services to the end consumer. We are their customers, and it is us who feed their power. Therefore, we have more leverage than we realize.

In the coming sections, we will go deeper into these ideas and how to implement them in a practical way. Tackling a problem this huge can feel overwhelming, and so it is important to remember that every drop does count. With every decision you make and every action you take, you are filling a bucket on one side or the other. It is up to us as RLSs to make sure we fill more of the survival and sustainability bucket than of the mass death and destruction bucket.

PART 3:
ONE-TO-ONE COMBAT

"You're much stronger than you think you are, Trust me."
—Superman

THE PRIMARY BATTLEGROUNDS

> "80 percent of the effects come from
> 20 percent of the causes."
> —Pareto principle

According to the Pare to principle, 20 percent of our business activity is causing 80 percent of the damage. While this is not an exact science, there are certainly some industries, and some aspects of our own business, that are a lot more unsustainable than others. We just need to figure out what they are and what the easiest solutions are for reducing that damage as much as possible.

There are a few targets we should focus our attention on. Energy, transportation, raw materials, use of plastics, and food production (animal agriculture in particular) are all critical battlegrounds that need conquering if we are to create a sustainable future.

In the following chapters, we will look at how we can do just this. Some of the ideas won't apply to you, but many will apply to the majority of businesses.

The good news is that there is a lot we can be doing. Some of it low or no cost, some of it expensive in the short term, but which will pay off in the long term. Other things may reduce profitability, but is just the right thing to do and will certainly make us feel better about what we do.

Some will appear to have very minimal impact, others considerably more so. The ideas that appear to make little difference, I have included, as they are free and very quick to implement. They should, however, not be ignored. Never forget that every drop counts. While the tiny things in of themselves have an incalculably small impact, compounded over time and multiplied by millions or even billions of people, they add up to be something very significant indeed.

I suggest you set aside two or three days and give your business a sustainability makeover. Start now, the sooner you implement the ideas, the sooner you will start making a difference.

Can you seriously imagine Batman answering the Bat phone, and telling Commissioner Gordon, "Sure, I'll sort out the city's emergency. Just give me a few days while I finish pimping the Bat mobile, and then I'll be right over. Remember, we are in the midst of a planetary civil war. And in war, time is always of the essence. Every minute counts.

ELECTRICITY

> "I'd put my money on the sun and solar energy.
> What a source of power! i hope we don't have to wait
> until oil and coal run out before we tackle that."
>
> —Thomas Edison (1931)

Our dependence on electrical power is growing at a daily rate. It is hard for most of us to imagine a life without it (despite about 16 percent of the global population not having any[76]). For virtually every business in the developed world, electricity is a must.

Unfortunately, the production of electrical energy is estimated to create 25 percent of the global greenhouse gas emissions[77](along with many other pollutants). This is almost entirely due to the mining and burning of fossil fuels.

The amount of energy generated by renewables varies considerably from country to country, and the numbers are rather interesting. The USA now has the second highest energy needs (after China).In 2014, the USA produced about 14 percent of its energy using renewable sources.[78] At that time China was already generating over 24 percent of its power from renewables and ramping up their production of renewable power at a much quicker pace.[79]

Several smaller countries are already operating at close to 100 percent renewable (almost all from hydro power). These include Bhutan, Nepal, Iceland, Zambia, Ethiopia, and Norway.[80] The world's forty-seven poorest nations have now also all pledged to be operating on 100 percent renewable energy before 2050, some by 2030.[81]

The good news is that in recent years the cost of solar has decreased dramatically. In 2016 unsubsidized solar power finally became cheaper than coal, gas, and in some places wind. It was also 2016 that saw India scrapping plans to build four huge coal power plants, and replacing them with solar and other renewable energy sources.[82]

Even in Dubai, where fossil fuels are incredibly cheap, they have found solar to be a cheaper alternative. The tide is starting to turn, though we still have a considerable way to go before we see all our energy needs being met by 100 percent renewables.

It is easy to point the finger at the power companies and blame entire industries. We should pause to remember though it is us who consume their products, and ultimately our businesses are responsible for what we directly and indirectly use.

For Internet-based companies especially, there is an enormous unseen energy cost of doing business. We are often aware of our own office power bill, but we don't see the full impact of our online presence.

The energy required to transfer data adds up quickly. In a study by *The Guardian,* it has been estimated that one e-mail generates approximately 4gs of CO_2[83]. To round off the numbers in these estimates, a quarter of this is from the host server, a quarter from the ISPs, and a half from the end user's device.

The site owner never sees most of this energy usage, yet the visited site plays a huge part in the amount of energy consumed. Everything from site structure to the level of image compression used and the choice of hosting all play a part in the online carbon footprint.

So what can you do about your energy usage?

Change power providers: Many countries have power companies who only buy electricity from renewable sources. Often this is at the same cost as other vendors (or only marginally different).

While you can't guarantee that a renewable source produced every electron of energy that enters your building, you can be sure that every cent you give supports only those who are producing renewable forms of energy.

Change your lights: If you have not yet done so, make the switch to LED bulbs. They use a fraction of the energy, do not use heavy metals (unlike compact fluorescent bulbs), and they last up to 20 times longer than traditional bulbs. They are slightly more expensive to buy, but usually pay for themselves in three to six months at the most (and even the upfront extra cost is now minimal).

Depending on where you live, you may have no choice. Many countries have already started phasing out incandescent bulbs, with some stopping their import as far back as 2005.

Switching to LEDs is just one of those no-brainer actions. They even produce a much better quality of light than other energy-saving bulbs. If you are not sure where to go to get the best deal, check the resource section at www.ethicallymad.com/superheroes.

Use auto-sensing lights in some areas: In a perfect world, people would switch lights on and off as needed. But this is not a perfect world, and we are humans with poor memories and bad habits.

So in areas that get only short bursts of use, such as a bathroom, consider installing LED lights that turn on and off automatically. These are now only a little more expensive than standard LED bulbs, but use even less power over time (and making the switch is literally as easy as changing a bulb).

Turn off electronics properly: Electronics that are on standby are known as energy vampires, and for a reason. Even when they are switched off, they slowly suck and waste power.

By plugging all of your computers, monitors, and other electronics into power boards, it makes it quick and easy for staff to turn everything off with a single switch at the end of the day. An easy solution to avoid wasted energy and money.

Check the brightness of monitors: Many people have their monitor brightness up way too high. This not only consumes more power than needed, but also can cause eye strain and headaches. It does not take long to check, but is well worth it.

Put computers into energy saving mode: Again, a surprising number of people don't take this simple step. If you are just doing basic web browsing, e-mail, data entry or word processing, you don't need your computer to run at maximum speed. For general use, you won't notice any difference in performance, but you will reduce your power usage.

Clean your mailing lists: Huh? How could making my e-mail lists smaller be good for business or the environment?

As e-mail lists grow older, they become increasingly less responsive. By filtering out anyone on your list who has not opened ane-mail in the past three to four months, you surprisingly increase the number of e-mails that make it to the inbox, rather than the spam folder.

Some companies, such as Google, monitor your newsletters and e-mail promotions to see how many people open them. The lower the percentage of opens, the more mail will get filtered or directed to the spam can. Businesses that keep their lists clean enjoy up to 8 percent higher deliver ability rates, plus their mailing costs are lower.

But once again, this is not just about the finances. As mentioned before, an average e-mail is estimated to generate 4gms of CO_2. For bulk e-mail that is not opened, this amount will be lower, but still has a footprint.

Optimize your website: As with e-mail, transferring data costs energy. Most businesses I have consulted for have poorly optimized sites. Unoptimized sites have a higher than necessary CO_2 footprint, and reduced conversions. (Website conversions have been shown to be affected by just a few milliseconds of delay. The less optimized your site, the slower it loads. And the slower it loads, the fewer sales you make.)

Have an expert take a look to see if you can reduce your company's online energy footprint while increasing its profits.

Check your thermostat: Way too many businesses over-cool or over-heat their offices. By having staff dress more appropriately to the season (more clothes in winter, less in summer), you can avoid having to overly compensate for outside temperatures.

In 2005 the Japanese initiated their Cool Biz campaign that encouraged businesses to relax dress codes and set air-conditioning to 28C. Research showed that in the first year they reduced carbon emissions by 460,000 tons, and in 2006 this increased to a reduction of 1.14 million tons.[84]

(And of course, the businesses themselves benefited financially too, thanks to lower energy bills.)

Get plenty of office plants: A high concentration of office plants helps absorb CO_2, increases oxygen levels, reduces office noise, increases employee happiness, increases productivity (by up to 20 percent in some studies), and helps minimize the cost of air-conditioning bills. And they look nice. What more reason do you need?

Use shades or insulation in the office: Using window shades to reduce the sun's heat can increase the efficiency of air-conditioning, while good insulation can help enhance the effectiveness of both air-conditioning and heat pumps or other heating.

This may already be taken care of, but many offices I have seen could benefit from a bit of an efficiency audit. Take a look; if there is no room for improvement, then no problem. If there is, the short-term cost will be soon repaid.

173,154,624 kgs (381,740,601 lbs) of toxic air pollution produced in the US annually from the production of electricity.[86]

About **60%** of the US's arsenic and sulfur dioxide is produced by power plants.[85]

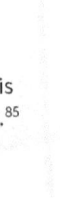

Up to **10%** of your **power bill** could be from your electronics on standby.[87]

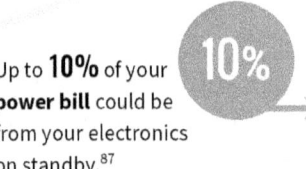

Electronic equipment on standby is thought to create approximately **1%** of annual CO_2 emissions.[88]

Almost **24 million** tons of coal used every day.[89]

An incandescent bulb will cost you **4-5x** the price to run an equivalent LED bulb.[90]

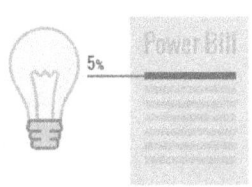

About **5%** of your power bill is for lighting.[91]

1.2 billion people still do not have access to electricity.[92]

TRANSPORT

> "A developed country is not a place where the poor have cars, it's where the rich ride public transportation."
> —Enrique Peñalosa

Transport has long been the scapegoat for climate change. This is a little unfair, though it does remain a major contributor to CO_2, along with a variety of poisonous gases. While nobody knows the exact number, estimates put transportation as being responsible for producing between 14 and 27 percent of the world's greenhouse gases.

From cars and motorcycles to airplanes and ships, the transport industry is heavily dependent on crude oil to power it.

Transportation is a huge piece of the overall problem, yet is crucial to keeping modern society functioning. Take even something as simple as food. One study estimated that the average American meal travels 1,500 miles (2414 km) to go from farm to plate.[93] Multiplied by an estimated 325 million Americans, and that's a lot of miles. (And that's just the food!)

Of course, it's not just Americans. Transporting food is a global issue. If we can significantly reduce the emissions from transport, we will certainly make a decent-sized dent in the environmental footprint of not only our food, but also our commuting, holidays, goods that we buy, and so much more.

It is estimated that transporting 1kg by air produces forty to fifty times as much CO_2 as it would by sea.[94] Unfortunately, that does not make shipping an environmentally friendly choice.

The shipping industry is responsible for tremendous environmental damage. It uses a filthy low-grade diesel as its primary fuel, which produces some very nasty pollution. It is estimated that the shipping industry is responsible for producing between 18 and 30 percent of global nitrogen oxide levels and 9 percent of all sulfur oxides (which form acid rain).[95] And despite not being as bad as transporting by air, shipping still produces around 4 percent of all greenhouse gas emissions, primarily in the form of CO_2.[65]

Shipping is also responsible for the death and injury of much marine life. The noise of shipping is thought to be severely damaging whale populations, and at just fifteen knots a collision with a whale has a 79 percent chance of resulting in its death.[65] Currently, there are less than four hundred North Atlantic right Whales left, and shipping is considered a major extinction threat.[65]

The environment is not shipping's only offense. It is also rife with social justice transgressions. It is standard practice for companies to register ships in countries with poor human rights laws so they can cut costs. Working conditions are often poor, and at times extremely dangerous.[96]

I consider myself to be a realist, not an idealist (therefore putting myself in the self-deluded majority). I know we are not about to suddenly stop shipping. In the long term, ships will likely be powered by solar and wind. However, as business owners and consumers, there is a lot we can do today to minimize the impact.

We all rely on shipping to some extent, whether it be sourcing our products or raw materials from abroad, providing us with food, or bringing us our cell phones and laptops. But by increasing our awareness, we can start to make better choices.

So what can you do to reduce the impact from your seen and unseen transportation needs?

When you upgrade your vehicles, consider going electric: Okay, this is hardly new, but it is worth it to point out, as many people still don't fully appreciate the difference.

A few years ago, this may not have been practical or affordable. Those objections may or may not still apply, depending on your needs, location, and budget.

Thanks in most part, I believe, to the sheer determination of Elon Musk, EVs (electric vehicles) are now set to become the default choice for the future. It may not feel like it yet, but we are much closer to all driving electric cars than most people realize.

The cost of EVs has fallen, the driving range extended (some equal to many petrol cars), and there are now many recharging points springing up all over the world—if you know where to look. And if you were not already aware, EVs are not a compromise, they are far superior in many ways.

Just in case you are not sold on the concept, here are a few points to consider:

- EVs can travel the same distances as many petrol cars on a single charge.

- They cost considerably less to drive per KM.

- They cost less to maintain (no oil, no clutch, few moving parts, less stress on the breaks).

- In some models, you get extra storage space where the engine used to be.

- They have better weight distribution and therefore better handling, as the batteries are spread evenly along the bottom of the car (whereas petrol cars have unbalanced weight in the front thanks to the engine).

- They are quieter (a major plus in cities where noise pollution is now thought to increase stress and be responsible for many health problems, even death).[97]

If you invest in a solar panel and charger, you can just about run your car for free. And with zero emissions.

If you plug into the grid to charge, then there are emissions created from nonrenewable power plants. However, power plants are far more efficient at converting fossil fuels into energy than a motor engine, so overall emissions are still considerably lower.

The current downsides(number of charging stations, speed of charging, and higher cost of vehicle purchase) are a consideration, but not as bad as most people imagine.

The upfront costs are easily offset in the long run, both through cheaper fuel and less maintenance. Charging stations are popping up at an increasing rate around the world, and for most people charging at home is all they would ever need to do anyway. Most small businesses with company vehicles can charge overnight and will have enough juice to last the day.

The downsides are being continually eroded overtime as battery technology improves and costs continue to decrease.

As a superhero, our job is to make the right choices. For many business owners, the long-term benefits, both environmentally and financially, mean that for many,electric vehicles are already the only logical choice.

Reduce your air travel: It is common knowledge that air travel produces huge emissions. Of course, we are not about to stop flying. But there are a few things we can do while we figure how to make alternative fuel powered aircraft.

The first obvious step is to reduce the frequency and distance we fly, where possible. Try having that meeting over Skype instead of flying, or ask yourself if you really need to go so far for your vacation?

For those who travel the long haul by business or first class, be aware this is estimated to generate between 2.5 and 5.5 times the emissions of flying economy.[98]

As part of their commitment to cut carbon emissions, some companies have already stopped using business class. (An easy decision when it is so good for their bottom line too.) If you fly first or business class, you may ask yourself the reason for your choice. Is it valid? Or are you self-justifying? An RLS must learn to be honest with themselves, and then act accordingly to their principles.

Source locally: Where possible, look for source materials closer to your manufacturing facilities and have production located as close as possible to the majority of end consumers. Often this won't be possible or financially feasible. Other times it will be just a matter of being more conscious about your choices, or you may need to sacrifice a little of the profit margin. This will be another chance to test your ethical strength as an RLS.

Teleconference when you can: There are many ways to reduce your footprint when traveling, but not traveling is the best way of all. It is the cheapest and by far the most energy efficient.

Thankfully free teleconferencing is now a practical option, giving us a simple solution to reducing at least some of our travel needs.

Allow people to work from home: The average commute time in the US is 25.1 minutes.[99] That's almost four and a half hours of driving to and from work every week. It is not uncommon for some people to be doing two or three times as much though.

If you help people avoid the commute (especially those living further away) you can reduce the net impact your business makes. The good news is that, counter to popular belief, employees have been shown to be more productive the further away from the boss they are.

Of course, depending on their role this will not always be possible. However, many positions can at least be scheduled so employees only need come to the office two to three days a week instead of five. Or, simply offering flexi-time gives staff the option to avoid traveling during rush hour, reducing both their stress and their carbon footprint.

Provide bonuses for eco-commutes: Knowing that the net impact of your business includes employees' daily commute,you could consider offering incentives for people to travel in more environmentally conscious ways.

Methods you may want to encourage include walking or cycling to work, taking public transport, ride sharing, or using electric vehicles. You could offer preferential parking, bigger company discounts, cash bonuses, public praise, or an extra day's holiday. Just don't offer a bonus that has a greater carbon footprint than the reductions made from the improved commute!

Consider your office location: Some businesses must be located in a particular place (such as your local main street). Others can be more selective as to where they locate.

If you can, locate your office in smaller towns or closer to suburban areas. This will reduce commute times for those who must work in an office, and often gives you the added advantage of lower office rent.

Flying **business class** has a carbon footprint **2.5-5.5x** bigger than flying **economy**[100]

On average driving a **petrol car** is **3x** more expensive than **electric**.[101]*

* Based on $4/gallon gas prices

The average New Zealander emits **3,240 kgs** of CO_2 per year just from driving petrol cars.[102]

The average American drives **26,634 km**/year (16,550 miles).[103]

In Western Europe transport generates **25%** of the pollutants that cause **acid rain**.[104]

The average American meal travels **2,414 kms** (1,500 miles).[105]

In 2009, the largest **16 ships** produced as much sulfur dioxide as all the world's cars put together.[106]

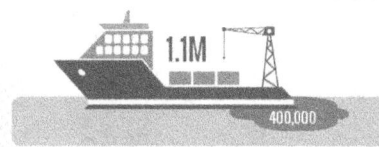

Annually an average of **1.1 million** tons of oil are discharged by ships, and another **400,000** tons are spilled.[107]

PLASTIC

"There is no such thing as 'away'.
When we throw anything away, it must go somewhere."
—Annie Leonard

Plastic is one of the best and one of the worst things to have come out of the twentieth century. It is one of the cheapest and most versatile materials ever created. It is, in its current form, also one of the most unsustainable and environmentally damaging.

Most plastic is made from either oil or natural gas. The extraction, transportation, and refinement of these fossil fuels causes a range of poisons to be released into the air, waterways, and ground. Once in use, many plastics continue to degas for weeks or months, releasing more toxic gases into the user's environment.

Of the 57m tons of plastics produced in Europe annually, 39 percent are used in packaging alone[108], and in the US approximately half of all plastic is used for disposable products or packaging.[109]

Once thrown away (which is often sooner rather than later—an average of only twelve minutes of use for a plastic bag), plastic can cause a range of hazards. Larger pieces can strangle or choke wildlife,and once broken down plastic creates tiny pellets that end up in waterways. These tiny pellets then poison the fish that mistake them for food.

But it is not just the plastic that gets thrown away. A recent search of UK beaches found lentil-sized plastic pellets known as nurdles washed up on 73 percent of shores examined[110]. In Cornwall, 127,500 pellets were found in a single 100 m stretch of beach alone.[75] These nurdles are used to makes plastic products, but it is thought that billions escape into the oceans every year—before they even have the chance to become something useful. Each time we use plastic we are unwittingly supporting this insane wastage and pollution.

While more and more plastic gets labeled as recyclable, this often does little more than make people feel better about using (and then disposing of) plastic. The harsh reality is that a vast majority of it never gets recycled, even if it is sent to a recycling center. Globally we are only recycling a very dismal 14 percent of all plastic.[111] A lot of what is recycled is first shipped off to China (requiring more fossil fuels to transport it), where it is melted for repurposing (producing more toxic gases). Once recycled, unlike metal or glass, plastic cannot be recycled indefinitely. Each time it is used the quality of the plastic deteriorates, resulting in lower and lower grades of material, until it can no longer be used at all.

As a planet, we have a finite amount of oil and natural gas. Despite this, we continue to use it on a massive scale to produce large quantities of plastic, most of which will be tossed away after being used only once or twice, after which it can take decades or centuries to break down. This information is unlikely to be new to you, but being honest with yourself, what have you done about it so far?

As business owners, we like to consider ourselves intelligent. As humans, we like to consider ourselves compassionate. Yet our use of plastic is neither intelligent nor compassionate. Current use either reflects a lack of education, or requires a strong dose of blame and self-justification. Something we are all too good at. However, an RLS does not sit back and assume that this is all someone else's problem.

There are alternatives to plastic in many cases. The question is, do we choose to pay the extra cost? Many small- and medium-sized businesses are choosing the costly alternatives and still surviving, so it can be done. (They too could, like most businesses, save money by using cheaper plastic alternatives. But these businesses understand the true cost of plastic and instead choose to put people and planet before personal profit.)

So as an aspiring superhero, what can you personally do?

Reduce usage: Firstly, avoid using plastic wherever possible. Do not substitute that which can be eliminated and was never really needed in the first place (a common theme throughout this book). If you are currently selling any products, look for ways to reduce the amount of packaging you use. If you are buying from suppliers, ask them if they can lessen the volume of packaging they use when they send you their goods.

Every industry is different, so this won't always be possible. But most people simply don't ever think about it. We have become obsessed about multi layering plastic packaging on so many goods. Companies who have taken the time to audit their packaging have often found that it can be significantly reduced with no compromise needed, and with the benefit of financial savings.

Make better packaging material choices: This will depend a lot on what type of business you run, but most businesses use some kind of packaging, even if it is just the bags they give to customers, or the envelopes they use to send invoices. The materials we choose to use to produce this packaging can make a big difference.

Talking of envelopes,I am continually frustrated by businesses and organizations (especially government departments) that insist on sending letters in envelopes with plastic windows. I get that it is more cost efficient not having to print and match the address on the envelopes, but it does make recycling much harder and is just another example of an unnecessary use of plastic.

In reality, most of these envelopes never do get recycled and end up in a landfill, leaving them to become another source of methane as they decompose. Many businesses use windowless envelopes without any problems. It may seem like a small detail, but when you consider how many of these plastic window envelopes get sent globally, it adds up quickly.

As for other forms of packaging, there are a few questions to consider:

- Are your packaging choices made from recycled materials?

- Can they be recycled easily once used?

- Can they be composted?

- Could the amount of packaging be reduced?

- Do you even need it at all?

If you do need to use packaging, then consider paper or glass. While not perfect,these material scan leave a much smaller toxic imprint and are far better for recycling than plastic.

There is also an increasing range of bioplastic alternatives. Many of these are not without fault, but I think in the long term most provide a far better solution than their fossil fuel based counterparts. Bioplastics have three noticeable advantages over traditional plastic: they are less toxic, often produce fewer greenhouse gases, and come from renewable sources.

One of the main criticisms of bioplastics is that many recycling facilities are not well equipped to manage them. Unfortunately, this is a bit of a short-sighted argument. Until they become the standard choice for packaging, there won't be enough in circulation to make them financially viable to recycle. The sooner companies start using bioplastics, the quicker recycling facilities will catch up.

The other complaint is that they use vast areas of farmland, and some are made from GM crops. These are more valid concerns, but ones that will soon need addressing—oil and natural gas are running out. As they begin to run low, their cost will increase to the point of making fossil fuel based plastics economically unviable anyway. Surely it makes more sense to find and use better solutions now, before we are forced into a toxic corner.

Some companies offer a range of bio-packaging solutions, so give them a call and see how they can help.

Use packaging that is designed to be reused: Some companies choose to use glass bottles for soft drinks, and in some parts of the world the price of each drink sold includes a small deposit for the bottle. Typically around 5–10¢.

This deposit is to encourage returns so the bottles can be reused rather than recycled. If the deposit is large enough, it can boost bottle returns up to ninety percent or higher. In Germany they are even using this concept for plastic bottles.

Deposit schemes could, of course,be used for multiple types of packaging. Shopping bags, supplement bottles, computer boxes, wine bottles, courier bags, etc.—the list is almost endless. It just requires a little thought and in some cases a better choice of packaging design.

Reusing packaging is almost always a better option than recycling it. And a little financial incentive goes a very long way in getting consumers to return it. Studies in the US have found that in states who use a 5¢ deposit per bottle, return rates were typically between 70 and 80 percent. When a 10¢ deposit is used,return rates can be over 95 percent. And remember, a deposit is not the same as a tax. It costs the consumer nothing extra, so long as they return the packaging. And companies benefit by saving money, as it is cheaper to reuse a bottle than pay for a new one.

Avoid the disposable culture: I know, disposable coffee or water cups are cheap and convenient. But even most paper ones are still lined with plastic.

If you provide disposable cups for staff, then stop. Replace them with real cups. For centuries people have managed to wash their cups after having had a drink. It won't kill them to do the same again.

Charge for packaging: People often take what is free without ever considering whether they really need it. Countries and cities around the world have already enforced shops to charge a small fee for plastic bags, and the results have been incredible.

Not only has the use of plastic been reduced, but it is better for the businesses too, as it is one less cost they need to bear.

Change the way you ask: If you must provide plastic bags as part of your business, then train staff to ask, "Do you NEED a bag today?"

Rather than just assuming a customer wants one or even asking, "Do you WANT a bag today?" It is possible to reduce the number of bags used greatly. A simple solution, and one that can save you money too.

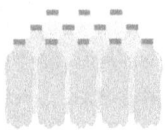 We produced more **plastic** between 2000 and 2010 than in the entire history of the planet prior to that.[112]

In the past 25 years, **10%** of all dead animals found on beaches were entangled in **plastic bags**.[113]

Microplastics are consumed by **zooplankton**, entering the food chain before eventually being consumed by us.[114]

 It is thought that it will take over **1,000 years** for a **plastic bottle** in a landfill to degrade.[116]

An estimated **4.8** to **12.7 million** metric tons of plastic end up in the oceans annually.[115]

Americans alone use **50 billion** plastic water bottles every year.[117]

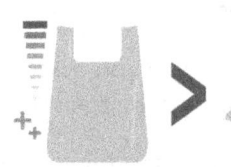

 Approximately **50%** of all plastic is used for **single use** purposes.[118]

If nothing is done, the world's oceans will have **more plastic than fish** by **2050**.[119]

ANIMAL AGRICULTURE

> "Our dependence on meat is one of the greatest climate threats."
>
> —**Alicia Silverstone**

Meat must be the proverbial elephant in the room. And due to the amount of industry money and the level of consumer emotion involved, undoubtedly the most controversial. Alicia Silver stone may be right about the threat meat has on climate change, but she is wrong about one thing: we don't have a dependence on meat, we have an exaggerated sense of entitlement to it, bordering on addiction.

I warn you now, if you enjoy your meat or dairy this chapter will be difficult to swallow. You are almost certainly going to find yourself becoming defensive. I urge you to read on with an open and impartial mind. I am only sharing the facts, which are what they are regardless what type of food you happen to enjoy. So please, don't shoot the messenger!

Estimates vary widely, but somewhere between 18 and 51 percent of all greenhouse gases are produced as a result of animal agriculture. Unfortunately, this is just the tip of the iceberg. The extent of its environmental impact is complex and difficult to comprehend fully.

I will only skim the surface of the problem here, but hopefully it will give enough information to help you understand that it is going to take an army of Real-Life Superheroes to act fast.

There are a few problems to be dealt with. The first, methane, is reasonably well-known. Animals produce methane; cattle, in particular, a lot of it. The average cow will produce between 70 and 120 kg of methane per year.[120] Your beef burgers, steak, and milk all come from giant methane burp and fart machines. And they require a lot of space.

Measured over a twenty-year period, methane is estimated to be approximately eighty-six times more damaging than CO_2.[121] This means that one cow over one year will cause the equivalent global warming impact as 8,600kg of CO_2. The same amount as produced by driving around 40,000kms in an average car.

But it is not just the CO_2 and methane. Animal agriculture produces over four hundred different harmful gases.[122] These gases include nitrous oxide, particulate matter, endotoxins, hydrogen sulfide, and around 80 percent of the ammonia found in the US.[86]

Next, there is the issue of land usage.

It is believed that over 70 percent of the Amazon's deforestation is to provide land for raising cattle,or growing crops to feed cattle.[123] And it is not just in the Amazon. Globally agriculture is thought to account for 80 percent of total deforestation.[124]

As a planet, we are faced with ever increasing CO_2 levels. Trees are one of our best lines of defense, yet we are destroying them at an incredible rate (an estimated three to six billion every year).[125]

When you calculate the amount of land required for grazing, and the additional land to grow crops to feed cattle,a meat eater requires eighteen times the land area to feed himself as compared to his vegan friend. And if you think grass-fed cows are more eco-friendly, think again. They require even more land than their grain-fed counterparts.

Then there is the issue of water. Forget for a moment the insane amount of fresh water required by animal agriculture (thirty-four to seventy-six trillion gallons annually in the US alone[126][127]). A much bigger problem is the water pollution caused from animal effluent.

This thick, smelly soup is poisoning our rivers and oceans, as well as creating dead zones where little aquatic life can survive. The knock-on effects from this are worthy of a book on their own, but needless to say, something needs to be done.

We have not yet mentioned the vast array of chemicals, hormones, and antibiotics that are now polluting our environment and our bodies thanks to the meat and dairy industry. Nor the various moral and ethical considerations.

Here is a simple fact: as a species, we can live healthy lives on a vegan diet. But pollution makes us sick, and we cannot live without rain forests—period.

Side note: If you don't believe we can be healthy on a meat and dairy-free diet, then time to do some research. Look at the evidence, not the propaganda from the meat and dairy boards. There are many millions of people who are living proof that without a doubt we can be vegan and incredibly healthy. From top Iron man athletes and mixed martial artists to the Seventh-Day Adventists who have some of the longest lifespans in the world, there are millions of vegans disproving much of what we were conditioned to believe about a "healthy" diet.

A 2012 Harvard University study found people who ate just 1.5 ounces (42.5 gms) of red meat daily were more likely to die early deaths than people who ate less than that.[128] A more recent study published in the BMC Medicine journal looked at 448,568 people from ten European countries. It concluded that those who ate the most processed meats (e.g., ham, bacon, sausages, and packaged meats) could expect an early exit from the mortal realm—that is, their lives were significantly shortened.[129]

This may be uncomfortable to hear. We may try to turn a blind eye. We may justify our decision or right to consume meat. But none of this will do anything to change the facts, or the consequences of continuing as we are.

James Cameron summed it up the best when he said, "The single biggest thing an individual can do is to shift more toward a plant-based diet. It's a win-win. It's a win for your health. It's a win for the environment."[130]

On one level the solution is very simple. Dramatically cut back (or better still, cut out) our consumption of meat and dairy. The reality, of course, is that for now at least, not enough people will willingly do this of their own accord.

John Reganold, a Regents' Professor of Soil Science and Agroecology at Washington State University, has calculated the numbers. He found that even with the estimated population of 9.4 billion by 2050, we can feed everyone on a vegan diet without destroying more forests or increasing farmland.[131] Other researchers from the University of Oxford in the UK found that, if the world were to go vegan, we would reduce farming emissions by a full 70 percent.[132]

This is easy to understand when we look at the following chart:

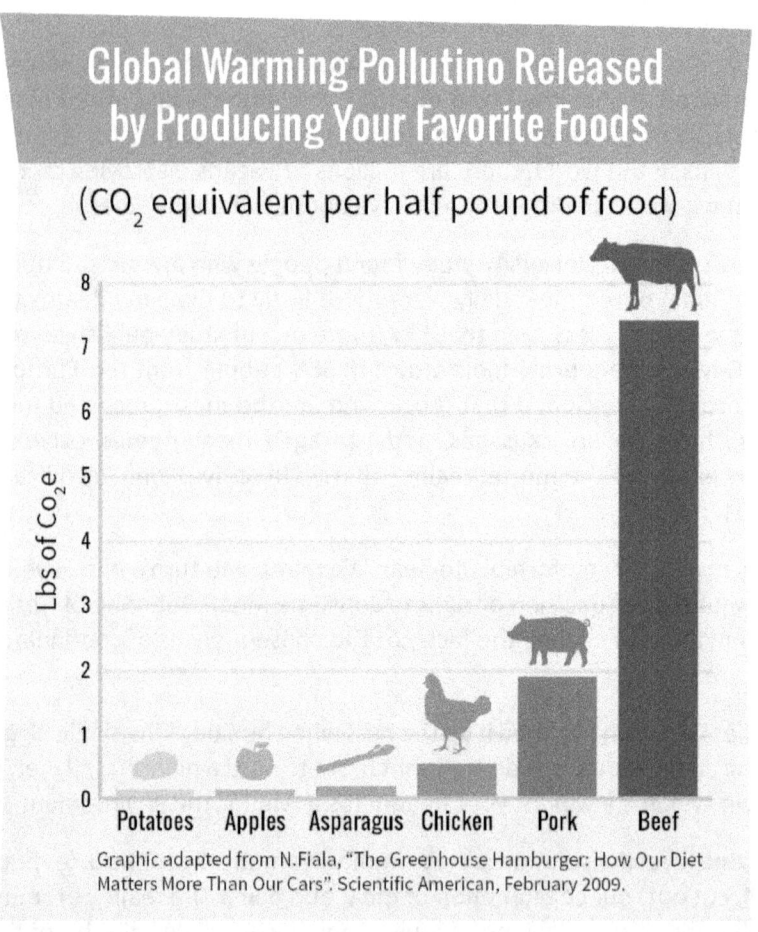

Global Warming Pollutino Released by Producing Your Favorite Foods

(CO$_2$ equivalent per half pound of food)

Graphic adapted from N. Fiala, "The Greenhouse Hamburger: How Our Diet Matters More Than Our Cars". Scientific American, February 2009.

If we continue a meat-based diet at the current level of Western consumption, we will have no hope. As Asia and Africa catch up economically, their demand for meat is also increasing. Currently, on a global level, only a privileged minority can afford to eat significant quantities of meat and dairy, and we are still struggling to meet even this demand (hence the continued destruction of virgin rainforests to try to keep up).

So, what can a Real-Life Superhero do about it?

As an individual the answer is obvious. Reduce or remove meat and dairy from your diet. I am not suggesting you have to give them up completely. But we have lost track of what is a healthy amount, or what is an environmentally sustainable quantity per person.

Pause for a moment. If you are a meat eater, chances are you are currently experiencing mental and emotional resistance. This is normal. Try to step back and look at it from the perspective of a visiting alien rather than someone who has spent their life eating meat. Identify the objections in your head, and check if they are actually valid. Remember, we are ninjas at self-justification. As an RLS we must become equally skilled at identifying and combating this mental excuse-making process.

For example, one argument I often hear is eating meat makes people happier. While I can't argue that many people enjoy eating meat, I can argue that eating more has not made us happier. Since 1970 the average amount of meat and dairy consumed has increased significantly, our life satisfaction has remained the same (though interestingly, heart disease and cancer rates have shot up in direct proportion to this increased intake of animal protein). I might also suggest (quite bluntly) that even if it were true, this is a relatively selfish and weak argument for justifying such enormous environmental devastation.

Meat and Cancer How Strong is the Evidence?
IARC CARCINOGENIC CLASSIFICATION GROUPS

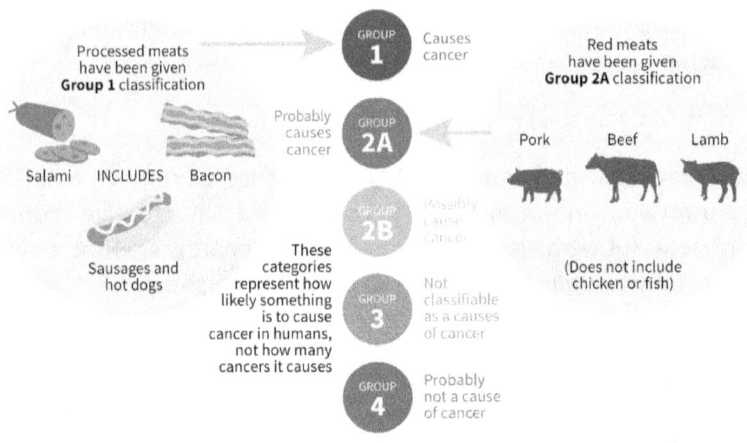

133

Back to what you can do . . .

As a business owner, it depends on what type of business you are in as to how much you can contribute to this particular fight. Here are a few suggestions that may or may not apply to you:

Restrict or remove animal based foods: If you provide any form of food for your staff, then you can become proactive by selecting very carefully what is on offer, and explain why.

If you are a café or restaurant owner, then consider looking for ways to dramatically reduce the amount of meat (especially beef) and dairy used, and offer more vegan options. People are rarely conscious of eating vegetarian or vegan food, unless it is pointed out to them. The truth is, meat eaters love vegetarian and vegan food; often they just don't realize it.

The more that both consumers and restaurants demand organic, plant-based foods, the more businesses further up the chain will be financially persuaded to change.

Educate others: The real power of businesses in the food industry is their ability to educate through marketing.

Organic food has been driven more by marketing than by natural demand. Yes, a foundation of consumers did create an initial demand, but it was the power of mass marketing that expanded that demand into a multi-billion-dollar industry.

If a business makes the decision, it can influence consumers in a positive way. Sure, it is easier to sell people on burgers and ice cream, but it is also perfectly viable to build a business selling people foods that are better for their health and the environment. Many businesses already do, it's just a matter of choice.

Create a new company culture: Another option is to try to encourage a company culture of one meat-free day each week.

A typical hamburger leaves a footprint of around 2.4kgs of methane, and between 0.67–2.2kg of CO_2, depending on how it was cooked.[134] Given that many estimates have put the power of methane as a greenhouse gas at as much as eighty-six times higher than CO_2 over twenty years, this would put a single hamburger's total equivalent impact at over 200kgs of carbon per burger. Insane!

Encouraging employees to go meat-free one day a week can help make a difference. It also creates greater awareness and potentially influences them to make other changes in their life.

Compost: Although not strictly related to animal agriculture, this suggestion is food related, so I thought I would include it here. More and more workplaces are providing recycling bins for their business and employee waste, but few offer a composting option.

When organic waste, including paper, is sent to a landfill site it breaks down using a mostly anaerobic process. This produces far more methane than an aerobic process (which is the process that takes place in a properly managed composter).

In simple terms, sending organic waste to the landfill will cause much more methane than composting. This is significantly worse than the relatively small amount of CO_2 that is produced during natural composting.

Change farming methods: It is the farmers that have the greatest responsibility and have the power to make a real difference, though it won't happen overnight. There are already many proven models for making farms more environmentally sustainable (while remaining financially viable). As each farm is different, it will depend on the climate, size, and soil type as to which model is best for any individual farm.

This is, of course, a topic that needs many books to cover. It is easy to make excuses as to "why it can't be done." The important point to keep in mind is that many farms around the world have already successfully converted from industrial farming practices to organic and permaculture methods.

It takes more than **18x** the land to feed a **meat eater** versus a **vegan**.[135]

Animal agriculture is responsible for **91%** of the **Amazon's destruction**.[136]

The **waste** from a farm of **2,500 cows** is equivalent to a city of **411,000 people**.[138]

90 million tons of fish are taken from the oceans every year.[139]

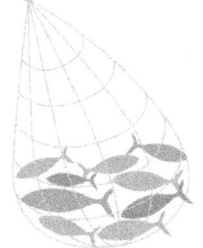

Every second a football-field-sized piece of rainforest is cleared for **animal agriculture**.[137]

Going from an **animal-based** diet to a **plant-based** diet can cut your carbon footprint by **half**.[140]

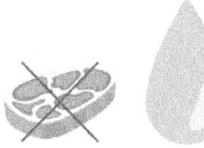

You can **save more water** by not buying **1 kg of beef** than you can from not showering for an **entire year**.[141]

One cow produces **120 kg** of **methane** every year **140–1000 times** more than a human.[142]

CLOTHING

Every one of us wears clothing, yet few of us give it much thought beyond the look, function, and price tag.

If you have watched the documentary *The True Cost*, however, you will be all too aware of the damage caused by the clothing industry. (If you have not yet seen it, I highly recommend finding the time.)

Many businesses are directly involved in clothing manufacture or retail, and others purchase uniforms, specialist clothing, or branded items. Sadly, most rarely consider the industry's footprint, and fewer still do anything about it.

Millions of workers continue to work as virtual slaves to keep industry costs low. Thousands have died, many more have been injured. Incalculable amounts of toxic waste have ended up in our rivers and oceans. More like a scene from a villain's master plan than business as usual for a superhero.

If you have just gotten a "great deal" on some clothing recently, you may want to pause before congratulating yourself too much.

How good would Superman have felt about himself if he were defending the innocent wearing a pair of red spandex undies made from sweatshop labor and whose industrial waste had poisoned innocent children and fish? Sounds a bit too melodramatic? I only wish this were just exaggeration. Sadly, this is the harsh reality for much of what we buy.

A real superhero would never stand for such social and environmental injustice. And nor should you. So, what is an RLS meant to do about it in the real world?

Buy from those who care: Thankfully from such a dark industry there are some glimmers of light. Outdoor clothing companies such as Patagonia and Kathmandu, and fashion brands such as People Tree and Indigenous are stepping up to try to change industry standards.

These companies are all working hard to source raw materials from sustainable, fair-trade suppliers, to ensure safe working conditions in the factories that manufacture their garments, to cut waste, and to reduce environmental pollution.

By supporting these companies, you not only reduce your social and environmental footprint, but you also send a message to other manufacturers by voting with your dollar.

Reduce the amount you buy: I have talked about reducing consumption already, but it is worth it to point out again. In the past twenty years, the amount of clothes we now buy has increased by 400 percent.[143] Perhaps it's all the new superheroes testing different outfits?

Buy quality, not quantity: This should be an ethos for everything. Clothing, in particular, has increasingly been seen as a disposable commodity. Buy clothing and footwear that is designed to last. My hiking boots are now twenty years old and have clocked up some serious KMs—so quality is still out there, you just need to be prepared to pay a little extra in the short term. It will pay off in the long term.

Look after your clothes: This is something we typically don't give too much thought to. However, washing too often, washing with harsh chemicals, or drying for too long in harsh sunlight will reduce the life expectancy of clothing. The faster they wear out, the more we need to buy. When you look after your clothes, you help look after your wallet and the environment.

In the past 20 years we have increased the amount of clothing we buy by **400%**[144]

In the **US 13.1 million** tons of textiles are trashed every year, and only **15%** are **reused** or **recycled**.[145]

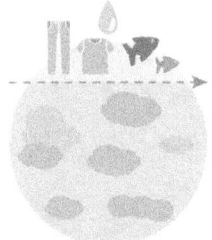

17%–20% of water pollution comes from **dyeing** and **treatment of textiles**[146]

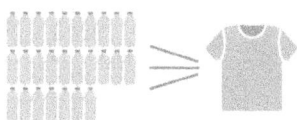

It takes approx. **2,700 liters** of water to produce a single cotton **T-shirt**.[147]

Conventional cotton takes up only **2.5%** of cultivated land but accounts for more than **16%** of the **insecticides**[148] and **16%** of the **pesticides**[149] used around the globe.

Only **2%** of clothing sold in the US is made in the **US**.[150]

The **Chinese** textile industry produces around **3 billion** tons of soot annually.[151]

The average person in **Manhattan** spends **$362/month** on apparel.[152] The average **Bangladesh** textile worker makes **$38/month**.[153]

RAW MATERIALS

> "A society is defined not only by what it creates, but what it refuses to destroy."
>
> —John Sawhill

Raw materials are usually so far up the supply chain for most of us, we forget even to look. From computers and other equipment to cars and buildings, indirectly every business relies on the supply of fossil fuels, metals, and wood, along with a host of other raw materials.

Just as consumer demands drive the direction of what we supply, so too does our demand drive the direction of our suppliers further up the line.

If we buy a computer, cell phone, vehicle, tools, furniture, even artwork for the walls, the raw materials all had to come from somewhere. And the choices we make at the bottom of the chain drive the demand further up.

As I have said before, we vote with our dollar; it is as simple as that. And what are we getting for our votes now?

Unsustainable logging practices, depletion of limited resources, pollution of waterways and oceans, massive loss of wildlife, untold suffering to families of low paid and poorly treated workers, along with a dangerous dose of corruption.

Awareness of the issue is the first step. But then what?

Some of the following suggestions will not be relevant to everyone. However, try to think how they may apply to you or how you may be able to modify the ideas to improve your sustainability efforts.

Stop buying new stuff: This is the most simple and effective solution to reducing consumption of raw materials and reducing wasted energy.

Yes, often we need to invest in new equipment or supplies for our business. But all too often these purchases are unnecessary.

Do you need the latest phone, computer upgrade, new car, etc.? It is estimated that over the lifetime of a laptop, 70 percent of its carbon footprint will be in making it, and only 30 percent in running it.[154] Chances are they can wait before being replaced. This gets more life out of your equipment, reduces environmental impact, and saves you money.

Not buying as much stuff is perhaps one of the best things you can do to help reduce your environmental footprint. It is the only truly non-impact strategy. Sure, often you will need to buy stuff, but developing a company culture of asking, "Do we really need to buy this?" will certainly help.

Buy second-hand: This won't be a solution for every item that you need to purchase. However, you would be amazed at how much businesses could save financially and environmentally if only they bought second-hand or repurposed products.

There is often plenty of old, quality office furniture on the market, as well as plenty of electronics that are just a few months old. Cars too can be purchased a year old, and many come with two to four years of warranty still on them.

Artwork, coffee machines, water coolers, plant pots, sofas, etc. You name it, the probability is you will find someone selling something that will do the job very well, and at a much better price than getting it new.

The great news, apart from cost savings, is that second-hand and recycled goods leave a much lower footprint. And let's be honest, after a while everything becomes second hand anyway!

Buy products made from recycled materials: When you are buying new products, look for manufacturers who aim to use as much recycled material as possible. When products use recycled material, they do not require virgin materials, which helps reduce the amount of deforestation or mining. They typically have a much lower carbon footprint too.

There is another advantage too. By creating a greater demand for recycled materials, you help support the recycling industry, pushing up prices and therefore increasing the economic viability of recycling waste.

Go paperless (or close to): A lot of wasted energy and raw material goes into producing paper. In the digital world, we can finally dispense with much of our dependency on paper. There are now many applications that allow documents to be signed online, and most B2B providers will gladly issue receipts or invoices online.

Advances in accounting software now allow businesses to go without that traditional mountain of printed paper, which is unnecessarily costly and time-consuming.

Give those service providers and suppliers who still send you physical mail a call, and ask if they offer a digital-only option. Many do, you just need to ask. If you are currently printing such invoices for your customers, then try offering a digital option by default.

Stop junk mail: Junk mail is another criminal waste of resources. There are two types of junk mail, addressed and unaddressed. Either way, both are costing you time (and therefore money), as well as being a burden on the environment.

Many people do not consider the impact of junk mail. Unfortunately, it is not only a huge waste of paper, but it also contains many heavy metals and poisonous chemicals. Much of it is difficult, or even impossible, to recycle (even if it does get carried away by your recycling company).

The best solution is never to receive it in the first place. To do this, try putting a No Junk Mail sticker on your mail box. This usually takes care of the majority of un-addressed mail. For those that are addressed, you can call the companies that are sending it to you and request to be removed from their mailing lists. In addition, many countries have an agency or service you can call to be taken off all unsolicited addressed mail.

For more information on why junk mail is not a good idea, and what you can do about it, head over to www.NoJunkMail.org.

If you are one of the guilty parties that currently sends such mail, don't be hard on yourself, but don't continue to self-justify this marketing strategy either. Many other methods are equally, or even more, effective. (If you are not sure how and need some help, then check out the list of sustainable marketing consultants in the members' area.)

Spam is unsolicited e-mail, even when it is geo targeted. Junk mail is simply unsolicited physical mail that has been geo targeted. It is time we phased out this outdated and environmentally unsustainable approach to marketing.

Change suppliers: Not every business is the same. Some are doing more to be socially responsible than others. And just as a shark's liver collects the accumulated poisons from further down the food chain, so too is your business an accumulation of the damage from further up your supply chain.

Many countries now offer lists of sustainably-focused businesses. By choosing to do business with others who are making an effort to use better raw materials, and to do the right thing, we can reduce the negative net effect of our own business.

These providers can include web hosting, e-mail services, telecom providers, couriers, manufacturers of computers and other equipment you may need, and suppliers of clothing, parts, packaging, or raw materials, etc.

Look for providers that are choosing to use renewable energies, switching to electric vehicles, manufacturing locally, ensuring proper working conditions and salaries for employees, sourcing sustainable raw materials, utilizing active waste reduction programs, operating zero carbon policies, and giving back to the community.

This will require a little research and is probably good to revisit every year or two, but doing so can make a big difference. Not only will you be lowering the net impact of your own business, but you will also be encouraging other businesses to continue their sustainability efforts, especially if you take the time to let both your old and your new provider know why you made the change.

If you head over to www.ethicallymad.com/superheroes you will find a list of different sustainability reports for various industries.

Find alternative materials: Specific solutions to every possible need would be impossible to fit in a single book and would be boring and mostly irrelevant to the majority of readers. But be aware there are a growing number of alternative solutions to many of our raw material needs.

I will share one of my favourites: hempcrete. In all my research, this for me is one of the most obvious replacements we should be using for many of our building needs. Hempcrete is an alternative to concrete, but as the name suggests, it is made using a blend of hemp, lime, and water.

Hempcrete is much lighter than concrete, is more energy efficient, provides better insulation, and is non-toxic, flame resistant, pest resistant, and water resistant. Oh, and it is also carbon negative, lasts an estimated four hundred years or more, and the build cost of a house is comparable to that of a standard home. Hempcrete is usually more expensive than concrete, but it replaces brick, concrete block, and other exterior finishes as well as the OSB, insulation, and drywall in traditional construction, which offsets the higher cost.

It is materials like hempcrete that should be making every business owner question their own industry defaults. If the construction industry is so slow to adopt a far superior solution than it currently uses, you may find yours does too.

A single **gold ring** generates **20 tons** of mine waste.[155]

Metal mining is the **number one** toxic polluter in the **US**.[156]

The **76,000 tons** of gold held by banks and investors would meet our current industrial needs for **186 years**.[157]

1,750 tons of soil and ore need to be removed to find a **1 carat diamond**.[158]

It is estimated to cost between **$5 and $15 billion** to restore Pennsylvania's waterways from the damage caused by abandoned coals mines' acid mine drainage.[159]

An estimated **600,000** children work in **gold mining**.[160]

The **mining industry** dumps **180 million** tons of poisonous waste into waterways every year.[161]

75.7 BILLION LITERS

64.3 BILLION LITERS

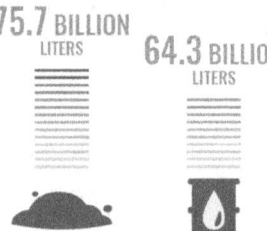

Drilling for oil has caused over **75.7 billion** liters of toxic drilling sludge and **64.3 million** liters of oil to be spilled into **Ecuador's Eastern Amazon** region and its waterways.[162]

REAL-LIFE SUPERHERO PROFILE

Business Name: G-Zen

Business Type: Restaurant

Founded By: Mark Shadle and Ami Beach

Year Established: 2011

Mission: To create tasty, healthy, sustainable meals that are a joy to eat, while caring for the environment.

Powers: Reduce the environmental footprint of eating out, create awareness of the environmental impact of food, support local organic farmers, and provide food that enhances the health of their customers.

The Story: Started by husband and wife team Mark and Ami, G-Zen is a fusion of their passions for food, health, and sustainability.

It is a restaurant that starts out with the belief that vegan food should be every bit as nutritious and tasty as non-vegan food. It also believes that we need to be making better food choices, not only for our bodies, but for our very future as a species.

To achieve their mission, they source only organic ingredients, and source locally wherever possible. They use Mark's years of experience as a chef, combined with Ami's skills as a holistic nutritionist and raw food educator, to produce a menu that is inspiring to the eyes, the tongue, and the entire body.

The results speak for themselves. They have received multiple awards for both the quality of their food and their sustainability efforts (including Travel and Leisure's "Best Vegetarian Restaurant in the USA," and Happy Cow's "Top Vegan Restaurant in the World"). This has obviously gotten them much attention, which has helped their marketing efforts significantly.

G-Zen proves that eating ethically does not have to be a compromise, and dispels the myths around vegan food being unhealthy, lacking in taste, or being only for dreadlocked activists.

Websites: www.g-zen.com

BALANCING THE FORCES OF GOOD AND EVIL

> "We make a living by what we get.
> We make a life by what we give"
>
> —Winston Churchill

As we have seen, despite the best of intentions and the best prevention and reduction measures, as a business we will still be responsible for doing damage to the world. It is, for now, almost inevitable. But that does not mean we can't do anything about it.

The most well-known method is almost certainly carbon offsetting, where companies pay to offset their carbon emissions. But this is far from the only strategy, and to focus on just carbon is a grave mistake. This is akin to having your attention diverted away from the full war by just one platoon (even if it is a very dangerous one).

Earlier we looked at the "Reduce, Reuse, Recycle" model. But I want to take a quick look at the fourth R, "Restore." The first three Rs are great at helping to minimize our impact, which is certainly important. But the reality remains that there are still negative consequences. Many people say this can't be avoided, and to an extent (certainly for now) they are right. But that does not mean we cannot take responsibility and do something about it.

Restoring is not a popular concept because it costs money. This is something that the stereotyped businessman or corporation hates. But that is not true for all, and for the sake of future generations we need to change this narrow mindset.

We must reduce our impact to a minimum, and start repairing what damage has been done as a result of our doing business. To be clear, this does not mean that as a small clothing brand you are responsible for cleaning up the devastation caused by the entire industry from every mono crop produced, every chemical used, every kilogram of CO_2 emitted, or every river polluted. But you can help clean up your fair share.

If each company took responsibility for cleaning up its own mess, there would still be plenty of profit to share. It just might mean that larger corporations only made $3 billion instead of $5 billion, and medium sized businesses only made $80 million instead of $100 million, while small businesses made $160,000 instead of $200,000. Like cleaning a house, the more people who help, the less any one individual needs to do. If we all took responsibility for our own mess and helped with the communal cleanup, the world would be a very different place.

In a later chapter, we will talk about how this approach has been used in the real world and how it can be used to generate free PR, help build a brand, and create brand loyalty, all of which can contribute to offset any upfront financial cost.

Here are a few ideas to get you started:

Plant trees: Let's start with the big one, carbon dioxide. Regardless of all the arguments, there are a couple of very simple facts. CO_2 is scientifically proven to trap heat (this is something that even climate change skeptics do not refute), and we have already unlocked more CO_2 into the atmosphere than has been there at any time in the past several million years (also unrefuted). This is food for thought considering as a species, we only evolved around 200,000 years ago, while the first signs of "civilization" were just 10,000 years ago (give or take a few thousand years, depending on your definition of civilization).

Now in fairness to CO_2, it is not the only greenhouse gas, but currently it does appear to be the largest contributor to global warming. The good news is that nature gave us two very capable CO_2 regulators: trees and phytoplankton. The bad news is we are destroying both at an alarming rate.

For a species that considers itself so intelligent, we really can be quite stupid! The Amazon rain forest alone is thought to produce 20 percent of the world's oxygen, and 70–90 percent of what has been cut down is just to supply more steak and beef burgers.

Forests do more than just help turn carbon dioxide into oxygen. They also help regulate temperatures in other ways, prevent soil erosion, reduce flooding risk, offer food and shelter to us and millions of other species, help bring deep groundwater up to the surface (allowing other plant species to survive), and so bringing the soil to life.

So what is the current suggested solution to this excess production of carbon combined with the current level of deforestation? Carbon credits.

The idea being that a company can become carbon neutral by offsetting its emissions rather than eliminating them. By buying carbon credits from an approved scheme, a company can ensure that the amount of CO_2 it generates is balanced by protecting an area of forest that would have otherwise been cut down, planting new trees, or utilizing some other way of offsetting carbon emissions.

On the surface, carbon credits make a lot of sense. While I think the idea is good in theory, in reality it has many flaws. Firstly, we are turning carbon into a commodity and allocating an "allowance" to different countries and businesses to create a fixed amount of CO_2. One way to offset carbon is to purchase someone else's allowance.

This is insane. We have already produced way too much. We are on borrowed time and can't afford for any business to be producing more. Whatever we produce, we must counterbalance, not offset through trading credits.

I am, of course, a big believer in protecting existing forests and think that is a job for citizens, businesses, and politicians. However, it has no place in a carbon credit scheme. We don't have enough forest to balance the CO_2 we are producing now. Thinking we can cause more pollution (which is already in excess) because we protect an existing resource that is already in deficit is just pure madness. They are both problems that need to be taken care of, but the current approach is not going to achieve the result we need. Not even close.

Another suggestion is to create a carbon tax. The idea here being that if businesses must pay for their carbon emissions, it will make fossil fuels economically unviable, and renewable energy far more competitive.

This would allow economic forces to guide businesses in a more sustainable direction.

The idea holds much merit; however, I think if we do impose a carbon tax, then that tax must be large enough and spent in a way that directly counterbalances the amount of carb on a business is producing. It would also be socially responsible for companies to pay a small additional surcharge to go toward preserving existing forests (as well as governments doing more to prevent further destruction).

Moving beyond carbon credits or taxes, the bottom line is we need to do more than stop cutting trees down and burning fossil fuels. We need to replant the trees and restore our atmosphere too. It is time to pay back our environmental debt—before we are made environmentally bankrupt.

I believe, it is the responsibility of every business (big or small) to do just that. Luckily, it does not have to cost the earth. But it will literally help save it.

There are now a variety of organizations that offer to plant trees for small donations. Founded in 1989, Trees for the Future is one such organization.

They developed a practical model that does more than just plant a tree. You see, the problem with many tree planting programs is that once planted, the trees are often neglected and die. Or if they do grow, they are eventually chopped down for firewood. Others focus in areas that, while successful, are cost prohibitive for real volume.

Trees for the Future supply seeds, equipment, and training to farmers in developing countries to help them grow fruit orchards. This ensures money goes as far as possible, and gives maximum social benefit. (And at a global level it matters less where trees are planted, so long as we plant a lot of them.)

Because the orchards provide food and income, it makes them more valuable alive than as timber or firewood. In this way, they have established millions of trees, as well as assisting poor communities to become more self-sufficient. And they achieve all of this at the cost of just 10¢ per tree planted. (Disclaimer: survival rates do vary from 10–20 percent, so the cost of each tree that lives is between $0.50 and $1.00. You can learn more about their work at www.trees.org)

Of course, Trees for the Future are not the only organization. There are many such initiatives out there; this is just the one I personally have chosen to align with and so know the best.

By building in the cost of planting trees to any product or service cost, it becomes very easy to offset your carbon footprint and help give back. Take for example this book.

An assessment carried out by the University of Quebec in 2012 found the carbon footprint of an average paperback was about 2.71 kg.[163] By giving 10¢from the sale of every book sold I can ensure that for every ten books sold, at least one tree will survive (hopefully two or even three.) According to the guys at Trees.org, who had a visiting scientist do the calculations, a typical fruit tree will absorb approximately 15.7kg of CO_2 each year for at least twenty years. This is a total of 314kg, or the equivalent of about 115 books.

Of course, there is also the transportation of the book, and none of this is an exact science. Even so, by giving just 10¢from each book, I figure the net result is at least leaning in the right direction. And it is just 10¢! Can I make more money not giving this money away? Sure. But do I need to? Of course not.

Also, if I use my marketing mind, it is easy to leverage this to help you, the buyer, feel better about your purchase. Some may call this a marketing ploy, but why not? It is a win-win for everyone and a long cry from the companies that use the words *natural or organic* in deliberately misleading ways.

There is hardly a business that I have come across that cannot apply this basic strategy. Imagine if every product or service in the world did this.

There were approximately 1.5 billion smartphones sold in 2016 alone.[164] Given the cost of a smartphone, it would not be difficult for manufacturers to build in a $1 charge that could be used to plant ten trees. With a 15% survival rate that would equal 2.25billion new trees. And that is in only one year! Within three years there would be one new tree for almost every person on the planet, and that's just from smartphone sales.

Clean the water: Water pollution is "the cost of doing business" for many industries. These include, but are not limited to,mining, oil extraction, agriculture, tanneries and textiles, and many manufacturing processes.

While there are strict regulations in some countries, pollution is still being created. In many other countries the regulations are minimal,or just not enforced. The results are sickness and death for millions of people, as well as the destruction of fragile ecosystems.

There are many projects that work to clean waterways or to enforce stricter policies to keep our waters clean. These types of project are often localized, and need as much financial support as they can get.

I encourage you to consider the damage that is done by your industry and where that damage is taking place. Then make an active contribution to help repair some of this negative impact.

Clean the land: Destruction of the land is happening in many ways. We are clearing trees, causing soil erosion, creating instability in the land itself (fracking, for example,is now a proven cause of earthquakes), and of course, poisoning the soils. Farming, mining, and waste disposal are just three of the most significant contributors to this problem.

There are a variety of organizations dedicated to protecting and restoring the land. While many are dedicated to trees in particular, others are working to restore our soils or to help educate farmers about more sustainable farming practices. Some local community groups are trying to remove industrial waste and toxins from their environment.

Help the sick: Sadly, millions of people are injured, made ill, or die due to poor business practices. While some people can claim compensation, many cannot.

As with most negative impacts from business, there are organizations trying to help. Like the others, they too need funding. By supporting these organizations, you help alleviate some of the social suffering caused by the darker side of doing business.

Protect other species: It is not just humans; animals have it even worse. The usual rate of extinction is 1–5 species per year. We are now losing dozens of species every day, which is between 1,000 and 10,000 times the natural rate.[165]

This enormous loss is directly attributed to the side effects of doing business. As an average business owner, you are unlikely to see these animals dying in front of you, so it is easy to have little awareness of the problem. But that does not mean we are not a part of it.

By giving back to animal conservation programs, we may not stop the mass extinction that is taking place, but we can do our part to help at least a few of the many amazing creatures to survive for future generations to enjoy.

To learn more about this issue, I highly recommend visiting the Center for Biological Diversity at www.biologicaldiversity.org and watching the documentary *Racing Extinction.*

Invest in the future: Thankfully, there are now many start-ups working to solve the myriad of business-related problems. They are developing solutions to provide cleaner energy, transport, food production methods, and more sustainable raw materials; providing drinking water; helping to reduce CO_2 levels; and making the world a more sustainable place in general. However, they too need funding.

Perhaps you can help give back by making a few riskier investments than usual. They may not all pay off, but if more people invested in companies that offered potential solutions, then the number that succeeded globally would increase. The more that succeed, the more options we have for improving the sustainability of our own businesses, and our lives.

As business owners, we are usually busy providing services and hopefully making profits. And many of us (at least claim) we would like to have time to help more. The reality is that, for most of us, business, family, and hobbies take up every waking minute. But we can still help by funding those who make it their mission to help clean up our direct or indirect mess.

"OUTSTANDING PEOPLE HAVE ONE THING IN COMMON: AN ABSOLUTE SENSE OF MISSION." - ZIG ZIGLAR

WHICH BRINGS US TO ZENBAGS

> "Setting an example is not the main means of influencing others, it is the only means."
> —Albert Einstein

Have you ever seen the tee-shirt or bumper sticker that says "Take my advice—I'm not using it." I am sure we have all been guilty of this on more than one occasion. While writing this book, I realized too much of the advice I was giving did not match what I was doing (something I confessed to earlier). So time for a fresh start . . .

It all began with an innocent conversation with a friend of mine. James, whose thick silver hair and wild eyebrows set off a beaming smile, has the energy of most twenty-five-year-olds, despite being squarely in his mid-seventies. (He assures me this energy comes from his decision to give up eating meat and dairy, and instead adopt a whole plant food diet. An extreme decision for an ex sheep and beef farmer!)

With his usual high levels of enthusiasm, he introduced to me to Linda (fondly known as the local bag lady), at which point they both began to try to enlist my help in finding a solution to reducing the use of plastic bags in the local community.

Of course, I was no fan of plastic bags. Certainly not the damage they caused, at any rate. If I am honest though, like most people, I subconsciously appreciated their practical utility and had more than my fair share that were taking over a kitchen drawer. But the more I turned my attention to the problem, the more I realized this was an issue that was crying out for an urgent solution.

This "coincidentally" happened while in the midst of writing this book, and so my mind was saturated with data and ideas. Here was an opportunity to demonstrate the principles of the book in a practical way and help save the world. And so it was that Zenbags was conceived.

The problem with the existing solutions we could find was that none of them were eco-friendly and most were not practical. This was despite all their "environmentally friendly" marketing claims. For example, most required that they be used 100–120 times before their carbon emissions became equal to the 100–120 disposable bags. Even organic cotton and hemp are not really environmentally friendly, as both require large amounts of energy to produce, and typically use unsustainable farming methods to grow the raw materials.

Another problem with these fabric bags is that they are much heavier. This not only requires more raw material to produce, but also makes them less practical. They are okay for getting a few items from the local store, but become bulky and heavy when you require ten of them to do a family shop. Even the reusable bags the supermarkets were selling proved too cumbersome to be very practical. So we turned our attention to the lightweight, fold able, reusable shopping bags.

You may have seen various versions of the design around. Many have little pockets you can tuck them into, and when compressed they take up little more space than your average plastic bag. This makes them easy to carry in your pocket or purse, and they weigh little if you are doing a larger shop. There were still some problems with this design though.

Most are made from virgin petrochemical based fabrics, usually polyester or nylon. While being quite energy intensive to produce, they were also difficult to recycle. And worse,they required virgin fossil fuels to produce. In truth, they were little better than the bags they were trying to replace. This was only made worse by the poor construction of the majority I investigated, which unnecessarily shortened their life span.

Then I came across an interesting fabric: RPET (recycled polyethylene terephthalate). This is a soft, durable, and lightweight fabric made from recycled post-consumer plastic bottles. Better still, it can be recycled again once finished with. This made use of existing waste, reduced the amount of energy required to produce each bag, and allowed it to be recycled into something else once it was finally finished with.

Now, let's be clear, this fabric is still not eco-friendly. Energy is still needed to produce and transport these bags. And in a perfect world, we would have no plastic bottles to make the fabric in the first place. But it was an exciting start. Once making the decision that this was perhaps the most eco-friendly, practical, and cost-effective material to use, the next stage was to design the product to minimize its impact.

The best way to do this was through designing the bags to last. The absolute opposite of planned obsolescence! This took some time, researching which would be the strongest stitching methods, how to reinforce stress points, and sourcing the best quality RPET fabric. Each of these revisions increased the raw cost of production, but only by about 15 percent in total. However, this is the 15 percent that many businesses try to cut to increase their profit.

Next, I needed to decide how to offset the energy required for manufacturing and transportation. I decided on the tree planting program through Trees for The Future which I discussed earlier. By planting a tree for every bag sold, we would easily offset the carbon footprint by three to four times, as well as contribute to the social sustainability of poorer African communities. In addition to this, we decided to donate a further 10 percent of profit toward helping clean and protect the oceans, as this was the one part of the planet that had been hit hardest by plastic bags.

To further reduce the impact of company operations, the main Zenbag office is powered by 100 percent solar energy, the servers are run on 300 percent wind power (helping offset even the energy used by visitors' computers), we run a paperless office, and our marketing is designed to help educate consumers to make better choices. We also ensure that the service providers we work with pay fair wages and have decent working conditions for their employees. As we grow, we will continue to work with our entire supply chain to keep reducing any pollution or chemicals used. (However, this type of leverage only comes with scale.)

Finally, as a distribution strategy, we decided to offer a partnership program to charities, nonprofits, and social groups we felt were doing good work. This enabled them to help promote us in return for a decent percentage of each sale being donated to their organization. A win-win for everyone.

As I said, this concept was developed while writing the book, so the business is still in its infancy, but we are already making significant progress. People love the idea, love the product, and want to get involved either as a customer or a distributor. Creating PR has never been easier, as there are so many newsworthy or interesting angles for journalists to use.

To learn more (or order your bag!!) visit www.zenbags.org.

I hope this case study inspires you to find your own problems to tackle. If every business took this approach, I have no doubt that the world would be a much better place.

PART 4:
GROW YOUR STRENGTH

"With great power comes great responsibility."

—Spiderman

WHEREVER THERE IS A PROBLEM...

> "When I am working on a problem, I never think about beauty ... but when I have finished, if the solution is not beautiful, I know it is wrong".
> —R. Buckminster Fuller

If I could summarize the mindset of a real entrepreneur, it would be this: wherever there is a problem, there lies an opportunity within its solution. For socialpreneurs, these solutions must be not only effective, but also beautiful. Physically beautiful if possible, but certainly socially and environmentally beautiful.

Countless entrepreneurs have built businesses that provide solutions to countless problems. In times gone by those problems were based on providing food, shelter, and transport. In more recent times entrepreneurs have focused a lot on finding solutions to increasing communication, comfort, and convenience. Now more than ever, I think we need to turn our creative intelligence to creating solutions for sustainability.

If you are an entrepreneur, you will risk your time and money developing a business that will provide some product or service. Why not spend this time and money wisely to develop goods and services that address the key challenges that we face as a society?

Many already are, but really, we need everyone to work together on this. Time is running out fast.

Does this mean compromising your ability to make money? No. Companies such as Tesla have shown entire industries can be profitably disrupted with greener solutions.

When asked what his most common piece of advice to budding entrepreneurs is, Richard Branson replied, "Do you have an idea that's

going to make people's lives better? If you do, you have a business."
[166] What could make more lives better than addressing the critical issue of sustain ability while improving, or at least maintaining, current standards of living?

I have attended many business seminars, and a recurring wish of participants is the desire to leave a legacy. Do you think you will be remembered fondly by society for leaving a financial legacy for a small few, which was achieved by destroying the planet? No. The greatest men and women in history are remembered not for their fortunes, but for how they shaped the world.

If you want to leave the ultimate legacy, then create sufficient wealth for your family while building a family name that future generations can be proud of.

Look around you. There are challenges and opportunities everywhere. We need to find solutions to more sustainable clothing, buildings, fuels, farming, electronics, and just about anything else you can think of.

There has never been a time in history with more opportunity for a true entrepreneur. Join us, and help retool business, finance, and the economy for sustainability. This is the age of the Real-Life Superheroes. You just need to start believing—in yourself.

REAL-LIFE SUPERHERO PROFILE

Business Name: Life Cykel

Business Type: Mushroom farming

Founded By: Ryan Creed and Julian Mitchell

Year Established: 2015

Mission: Enable people and the environment to grow healthier with mushrooms.

Powers: Reduce methane production from coffee grounds decomposing in landfills, reduce the carbon footprint of oyster mushrooms being sold in Australia, get people involved in their own food production, and raise greater environmental awareness.

The Story: Ryan and Julian, both still in their twenties, met while working full-time jobs in a remote mining town in Australia. Part of their job was to look after the health and wellbeing of the community, and to do this they realized residents needed to get access to more fresh food.

It was during this time they came up with the idea to grow fresh mushrooms using the coffee grounds that were being thrown out by local cafes and restaurants. They also knew that when organic matter enters a landfill, it produces methane. By keeping the coffee grounds out of landfills and using them to grow mushrooms, they could help close a loop.

Most of the oyster mushrooms that were being used in restaurants were coming from overseas, so this was a great opportunity to kill two birds with one stone. Reduce methane emissions from landfills and reduce CO2 emissions from food miles (a measure of the fuel needed to transport food from one place to another, per mile).

In October 2015, they successful crowd funded their startup, raising $30,000. Over the following months, they raised an extra $40,000 by using recycled exercise bikes connected to washing machine motors to power community cinema events.

They used this money to open Australia's first urban mushroom farm in Free mantle, just south of Perth. In March of 2016 their first commercially produced mushroom was grown. By July of that year both partners had quit their jobs to work full-time on the business.

In addition to the farms, they also produced mushroom grow kits for people to use at home. True socialpreneurs, Life Cykel has started distributing these home grow kits through schools to help the schools raise funds, while engaging families in growing their own food.

The schools have been enthusiastic to embrace a healthy, sustainable way to raise money. Traditionally they have sold chocolate, cookies, and cakes to raise funds. Now they can make money promoting something that is not only healthy, but educational too.

By August 2016 they had already expanded to Margaret River, and in September of the same year they had raised the money to begin operations in Melbourne and shortly after Noosa. They are in the process of expanding to New Zealand and plan to be global within the next three to five years.

Their efforts have not gone unnoticed. They have been featured on ABC News, Today Tonight, Startup Daily, and The Huffington Post, amongst many other blogs and news outlets. As Ryan will tell you, marketing is everything to a new business, and having a great story with a message that engages people has been crucial to their rapid success.

Ryan and Julian are two Real-Life Superheroes with a great business, making a positive difference. They love what they do and provide an inspiring example of how to make money while enjoying life and helping others.

Websites: www.lifecykel.com.au

MARKETING MADNESS

> "More brands are waking up to their social responsibility and doing good work through cause marketing campaigns. Yet too many still go about it the wrong way. I mean 'wrong' in two senses. Firstly, they are marketing ineffectively, and secondly, as a consequence their positive social impact is not maximized."
>
> **—Simon Mainwaring**

I would like to address another opportunity that contains a new dilemma: marketing yourself as "green." This is not a book on marketing, so I won't go into specific methodologies. But some underlying principles should be addressed.

A superhero needs to be careful. He or she must be seen as a humble provider of solutions. Not a fraudster or vigilante.

I have discussed this idea with many business owners and consumers, and there is a common concern that gets raised again and again. There is a feeling that the "green" card is overplayed, and all too often this is true.

Many companies market themselves as green because they use a recycled box or use an organic ingredient that makes up 0.1 percent of their total product. This, in my opinion, is highly unethical and should be illegal. It misleads consumers, and it trivializes the efforts of companies working on real solutions. Don't be one of these.

On the other side, you have companies like Kathmandu (headquartered in New Zealand) who do not market their sustainability efforts anywhere near enough. They have very active programs in place to make significant progress and are miles ahead of the local competition. Yet, even as a long-time customer, I knew none of this. That is, until I researched them.

It is not that they are trying to hide their good work. It is there on the website—if you look hard enough. There are some hints on their tags and labels, but you need to know the industry lingo to appreciate most of it. And they do release a company report with their latest progress for all to see. But how many of the general public ever read these reports?

No offense to Kathmandu, I have a lot of respect for them, but I feel they have dropped the ball on the marketing front with this one. For a start, they are genuine with their efforts and are doing an admirable job. They should be proud of what they are doing, and they have earned the right to brag a little about it.

Given that most outdoors people care about the environment and as a whole are very outdoors people, this is a point of difference that will certainly make sales. As a customer, I now feel proud to wear Kathmandu clothing. Before my research, it was just one of many options for outdoor clothing which had little to separate it from the competition intellectually or emotionally. Other customers deserve to make more informed choices and feel good about their purchases too.

But here is where I think their marketing can do the greatest good: by highlighting their efforts, they highlight the problems the industry faces. They create public awareness, and they help consumers care. This in turn puts pressure on their competition to also start doing the right thing.

Once a new industry standard has been adopted (for example,as with CFC-free spray cans), the marketing edge is lost and no longer required. Companies such as Kathmandu though are always pushing the boundaries. They are working to make their stores energy efficient; use recycled materials in their construction, sustainably sourced materials for their products, and ethical manufacturing; and are working toward a zero-waste operation.

On an international level, Patagonia is already famous for their commitment to the environment and to social responsibility. They have embedded sustainability squarely into their brand identity and the corporate DNA.

While it may not be necessary for Kathmandu to be quite so extreme with its company image, it could certainly do much more with its marketing efforts. I have only spoken to their sustainability coordinator, not their marketing team, so I can't comment as to why they have not gone down this route. But as a customer, I would personally like to see more information in their stores. Even if it were a simple large display poster with the key sustainability metrics they have achieved and goals they are working toward.

The best marketers understand the value of education. In the past, large companies have used this concept unscrupulously. The meat boards created the myth that we require large quantities of animal protein (now thoroughly dis proven, but still one of the most common food myths that perpetuate, even amongst many doctors). Dairy boards had us believing that the only way to get our daily intake of calcium was through milk— again a total lie (there is more than enough calcium in vegetables, seeds, and grains).

It is this type of deceptive behavior that has given marketing a bad name. However, let's not throw out the baby with the bath water. Good marketing is indisputably powerful and extremely effective. It is a tool that if left only to the unethical, will leave the average person severely misinformed.

As ethical business owners and socialpreneurs, we must learn to harness this powerful force for good. We can use our marketing budget not only to make sales, but also to help educate consumers to make better choices for themselves and the planet.

Depending on your industry and how quick to market you are on this, there is also a host of PR opportunities. Climate change is big news and sustainability is fashionable. This means the press loves anything that is new under these broader topics. If you are making changes to your industry, the media will likely print your story. You just need to make it interesting enough, and remember to tell them about it.

Another proven marketing strategy is affiliating with, and donating to, larger not-for-profit organizations who are doing good social and environmental work. With this type of affiliation,there is more potential for media coverage, exposure to that organization's members, and increased trust for your company brand through association.

Many ethical business owners struggle to take advantage of these opportunities for(ironically)moral reasons. This is crazy. It is a win-win-win opportunity that helps educate the public and raise money for organizations, and makes you more sales (which means more people are supporting an ethical company).

The danger in this comes when a partnership is formed and one side "sells out" for the cash (which can happen from either side). For example, an ethical charity may partner with an unethical business simply to get a handout. Or an ethical company may partner with a larger but unscrupulous charity for the exposure. Either way, it can damage trust or reputation. However, if both sides of the partnership are in alignment with each other, then both have plenty to gain with little (if any) downside.

There is another advantage ethical businesses have over traditional competitors: they are now able to get listed in a variety of sustainability directories and resource guides. There are even browser plugins and apps such as **www.donegood.co** that help consumers find suppliers who are making an effort to do the right thing.

Uninformed or uncaring customers don't mind buying from an ethical company (they are just unlikely to seek one out), but an educated, caring customer will choose to do business with one company over another based on their sustainability efforts. By being a socialpreneur, you may get loyal customers that you would not get if you were just a vanilla entrepreneur.

Investors too are seeing this trend. An increasing number of investment firms, pension funds, private investors, and even city investment funds are divesting from harmful businesses. Instead they are investing their dollars in companies who are making genuine efforts toward sustainability. To qualify for this investment though, you must first position your business as a sustainable solution. Ethical marketing.

I OBJECT!

Any good business owner will need to become familiar with overcoming objections to their product or service. This is perhaps even more important if you are leading a revolution in your industry, introducing something unfamiliar, or trying to get people to think in new ways.

And so, in this chapter, I will attempt to deal with some of the common objections (and often self-justifications) I have come across while writing this book.

What about free choice?

We have been raised to believe in the right to free choice. It is an argument that comes up again and again to defend people's right to continue as they are. Yet it has never actually existed.

Free choice has always been relative. Relative to where in the world you are, when in time the decision is made, your age, gender, and financial net worth, and a variety of other social or physical limitations. At the extreme, you have free choice to murder everyone on your street, but there will be serious repercussions, as society does not usually consider this an acceptable choice.

Not so long back, businesses were free to choose to use slave labor. That is no longer an acceptable free choice. So then, it could be argued that free choice is acceptable, so long as it does not harm another. But if we use this measure then, due to the negative impact that most primary industries have on the environment, and consequently on people, businesses should not be allowed to continue operating as they are.

If we buy meat, petrol, plastics, or other products that we know have caused harm to others, then we could argue that this should not be an acceptable free choice. Of course, it is not that simple, but the argument of free choice is often over simplified. Anything that challenges a currently available choice is deemed as a threat and is usually rejected without proper consideration.

Free choice is important, but it is not a justification that can be used by anyone for any action, including the purchase or production of anything, just because it is available and legal at any given point in time. (We will look at legality as a specific objection in just a moment.)

We must also consider the free choice and rights of others: the right and freedom to choose to breathe clean air, drink clean water, have access to organic foods, not have their lands or oceans depleted and made barren, and earn a fair living so they can provide for their families.

We may not see it, but many of our daily "free choices" are violating these free choices for billions of people around the world, ironically including us.

It's not breaking the law, so what's the problem?

Many people use "the law" to defend their choices. "It is legal, so what I am doing must be okay."

When faced with these arguments, it should be pointed out that the law is not a black-and-white reflection of what is right or wrong. It is an ever-evolving blend of social attitudes mixed with the beliefs and desires of those in power.

Laws are not fixed, nor definitive. They change depending on time and place. We have new laws that ban certain things (such as slavery and CFCs) that were once perfectly legal. And in the future, we will have laws that ban things that are legal today.

We do not need to wait for the law to change, before deciding what is right or wrong. Instead of waiting to be told what we can or can't do, we need to look beyond our own selfish desires before deciding whether something is acceptable or not.

What about people losing their jobs?

On the surface this argument makes sense, but it is only skin deep. If we were focused solely on preserving jobs in the short-term, we would never have had the agricultural revolution, nor the industrial or technological revolutions. Progress requires change. And change requires, well, change. That means some people will need to change what they are currently doing, i.e., some current jobs will need to go.

An economist (sadly I forget who), once explained it using roughly the following example...

Imagine an ancient island with a population of 1,000 people. For these 1,000 to survive, they must all be involved in daily hunting, fishing, collecting vegetables, and building basic shelters. Their methods are very primitive, and they have to catch each fish one at a time using only a sharp stick.

One day, Olgarth has a bright idea. He weaves the first net and is able to catch the same number of fish as twenty men. This effectively frees up nineteen out of every twenty fishermen, (as the island's population has little need for more than they can eat). So what happens?

These "unemployed" individuals are now free to focus on finding other solutions to the island's challenges. The excess man power can devise solutions in increasing farming yields, which frees up more people. They then design better tools to speed construction; this frees up even more.

If we had not removed the "jobs" of vast numbers of people, we would never have advanced beyond hunters and gatherers.

As a society, we should be more concerned with helping and supporting the transition of those caught in the latest progress, rather than trying to resist it. When it comes to change, over a long enough period of time, resistance is futile. However, exactly how that change takes place is something we do have a degree of control over.

Trying to preserve jobs in industries that threaten our future as a planet (e.g. coal miners), based on nothing but economics as an argument, is nothing short of foolishness. While intentions may be good, it would only be a short-term victory at best. Geoff Summerhayes from the

APRA (Australian Prudential Regulation Authority) has declared that climate change could threaten the entire financial system. If there is any industry that understands risk and finances, it must be the insurance industry!

With renewable energy now making so much progress, trying to save the coal industry is akin to trying to save the jobs of people who make fax machines, only with direr consequences. The longer we delay this transition, the more abrupt it will inevitably happen. This abruptness will cause more challenges than simply thinking ahead and putting measures in place to soften the necessary change and reduce the economic cost.

Businesses are only trying to meet customer demand, so surely we need to focus on getting consumers to change?

Yes, but more no. Take fisheries, for example.

Has there always been a demand for fish? It's difficult to know for sure, but let's assume yes. But what was the level of that demand? And is the fishing industry responding to that demand, or are they creating it?

With the advent of industrial fishing practices, the price of fish was dramatically reduced and profits increased. With lower prices demand naturally increased. With the higher profits, fishing companies could begin to invest more into marketing, and therefore artificially drive demand. You can be sure if advertising and marketing did not drive up demand, companies would not waste their money on it.

Steve Jobs claimed that Apple rarely did market research. They created things and then told people they wanted them. Apple created products, and then created the demand for them. Having a large customer base of people willing to spend money on something is not the same as filling a natural demand.

I worked hard, and I earned it, so why pick on me?

If there is one thing we have been brought up within the supposedly developed world, it is a sense of entitlement. We have become so conditioned by marketing and media to desire big houses, big cars, and big meals, that we have come to believe it is our birthright.

While I have no inherent problem with someone owning a large house, or a big car, or loading themselves up with huge steaks, it should be done with an awareness of the impact to others. Essentially this sense of entitlement has made us not only increasingly greedy, but also exceptionally self-centered and inconsiderate. When evaluating the impact that our choices have, we tend to only look at the surface, often only as far as our bank account.

The media has taught us that we can have whatever we want, so long as we can make enough money, or put it on credit. It avoids the more uncomfortable questions like social equality or environmental impact, and so we rarely give these things a second thought. But just because we don't think about them does not mean there is no impact. That is not to say we should not have big houses or cars, just that the culture of "bigger is better" has consequences that are largely unseen, or even thought about, by the consumer.

Any time our desires are questioned this sense of entitlement kicks in and we become hyper-defensive. Arguments often become driven by the fever pitch emotion of a cult, where logic and rational thinking struggle to penetrate.

It is time we became more intelligent, and instead of being jealous of or aspiring to lavish lifestyles, we should instead be asking questions about what these choices are doing to impact the lives of others and the very future of the planet. With this awareness, we become more considerate and begin to make better choices.

My priority is to provide for my family, so isn't what you are suggesting just idealistic fantasy?

This is an objection based on false logic. The same argument could be made by a jewel thief or a mugger. The argument of providing for your family does not take into account how you are achieving that goal. As we discussed before, this book is not concerned with what is legal, but what is ethical based on what is good for society.

There are two inherent problems with this type of thinking. The first is a simple false assumption that you can't provide for your family while doing something that is also beneficial for society. The second is in the broader context of "providing for the family."

Surely part of any parent's responsibility is to provide not only food and shelter, but also the best possible future for their children and future generations. This means not only generating sufficient finances to meet the family's day-to-day needs, but also doing so in a way that leaves the environment intact, does not deplete precious resources, and will not lead to social unrest.

It's too late anyway. What's the point?

As they say, it's not over until the fat lady sings. She may be warming up, but the final concert has yet to properly begin. That is to say, most scientists believe we still have time.

The flywheel is already in motion, and it will take time to slow down. It is too late for those individuals already killed by pollution, too late for the many species already extinct, and too late to prevent severe damage from climate change, but it is not too late to save the human race and many of the other life forms that share this planet with us.

Every day we don't do something, more people suffer and die, more species go extinct, and the more difficult (and expensive) it will be to prevent total collapse. Then one day there will be absolutely nothing we can do. The window of opportunity will be lost, and we will have no one to blame except ourselves.

If there is even only a small chance of success, then I say we should try. This is no longer just about future generations; it is about us today. And every day we delay taking action, the more extreme that action will need to be.

I find it ironic that we work so hard to try to prolong an individual dying person's life, usually at great expense, but we do so little to prevent millions dying from the global issues outlined throughout this book. As with many illnesses, prevention is cheaper, less painful, and often more effective than cure. If we deem necessary these inevitably futile efforts to save the life of one person (they will eventually die sometime, somehow anyway), then surely it is worth the effort to save humanity itself, despite the odds. And as every doctor will tell you, the sooner you start treatment, the better your chances of success.

Pollution and climate change are problems for the scientists and governments. What difference do I really make?

Regardless of whether you believe it or not, you do matter. You do make a difference. You are creating change, for better or for worse.

A lot of what is discussed in this book is very big-picture stuff, and many people feel like a small detail. But here's the thing: it is the small detail that makes up every picture.

Yes, governments have a responsibility to help provide guidelines for businesses to conduct business, and for citizens to live their lives in a way that creates a harmonious society. We should encourage our governments to make better decisions in this regard, and stop thinking of the economy as the number one priority, but we should also not rely on them to look after us like kindergarten teachers. We are adults, and we need to act like adults.

Scientists are great at identifying the cause of any given outcome and are good at using these data to predict future outcomes based on the laws of cause and effect. Sometimes they use this data to create forecasts of the future, and create a warning for us, other times they use them to develop solutions that create new technology.

Scientists are crucial. They help both governments and businesses to make better decisions and provide better solutions. However,the scientists themselves do not implement the changes they see needed in society.

As we have discussed extensively throughout this book, the negative impacts we see in the environment are almost exclusively a result of businesses conducting business. Every one of us makes a difference, but as business owners, we have the power to create more change than most.

If businesses start paying for their cleanup, won't products become too expensive?

The cost of goods will almost certainly increase if businesses start cleaning up after themselves. However, someone needs to foot the bill, and the actual increase in end costs need not be high (especially if larger companies reduce their profit margins). As mentioned before, we have a massive environmental debt we have built up, and paying this back will cost money.

So who should pay? If the companies that make the mess don't clean it up, then it is left to charities and governments. If charities do the cleanup, then it is paid for by the generosity of people like you and me. If the governments manage the cleanup, then it comes from taxpayers' money.

But is this fair? The business owners get to walk away with larger profits,and those who over consume pay the same as those who live more modest and lower impact lifestyles.

The longer we leave it before business takes responsibility for the destruction it is causing, the greater the repayments on our environmental debt will be. Those who are creating the debt should pay for it; anything less is simply not fair. This is not rocket science;most high school kids could understand this.

Would the economy not just collapse if we all stopped eating meat, driving cars, or doing many of the other things that are so detrimental to the environment?

If it happened overnight, then yes, of course. But this is not about to happen anytime soon. However, nor does it give those who are educated about the problems permission to carry on as they were.

Like any change or new technology, we need the early adopters to test the concepts, find the problems, and lead the way. This helps soften the blow to existing businesses and gives them time to pivot and restructure for the coming changes ahead. As the majority adopts these new ideas,the changes begin to have a significant impact, and momentum builds. There will always be a few "laggards" to provide an outlet for old stock and business in the final phases of reorientation, but eventually these too will catch up, and the transition to a new way of doing things will be complete.

Looking around to see what everyone else is doing before committing to change is exactly the type of herd mentality that is making essential progress so slow. The more people who require the majority to eat less meat or conduct business in a sustainable way before changing their ways, the sooner the masses will follow. But even this still takes time.

There will be economic disruption, this is inevitable. But the longer we all wait before doing something, the bigger that disruption will be. Therefore, this objection is clearly a weak attempt at self-justification to continue on a current path.

Isn't what you are suggesting a little extreme?

We have created a state of emergency. The damage already done is extreme. Don't be surprised if the solution is also extreme, but it is nothing compared to how extreme things will become if we don't do anything. Sticking your head in the sand does not make the problems go away—it just makes them worse.

"MOST NECESSARY EVILS ARE
FAR MORE EVIL THAN NECESSARY."
- RICHARD BRANSON

THE KEYS TO HAPPINESS (AND THE REAL-LIFE SUPERHERO'S TRUE STRENGTH)

> "Are you bored with life? Then throw yourself into some work you believe in with all your heart, live for it, die for it, and you will find happiness that you had thought could never be yours."
>
> —Dale Carnegie

Why do we want to make more money? When we get past the desire for a better home, more security, social status, more toys,etc., underlying all this for most people is the belief that more money will bring more happiness.

Sadly, this is severely misguided thinking. While it is true that alleviating poverty does help ease suffering, which in turn increases one's ability to be happy, past a certain point (i.e., enough to live an average life without financial worry) more money fails to influence a person's happiness significantly.

Comparing ourselves to others who have more does more to diminish happiness than reaching their level does to increase happiness. There will always be someone further up the chain, so this type of mindset (keeping up with the Joneses) actually makes you unhappy and will keep you in the rat race,endlessly trying to attain more.

So, what does make us happy? Living with purpose, helping others, and being congruent does help us enjoy our lives, and enables us to find greater peace in ourselves. This is something that the Real-Life Superhero may understand intellectually at the beginning of his or her journey, but once fully embraced, this ancient wisdom will become a source of their true power.

As it has been said, the happiest people don't have the best of everything; they make the best of everything.

I repeat, you will face many challenges and tests along your hero's journey. You will question your beliefs, your choices, and your abilities. You will be faced with temptations, and during these times you will need the strength of a superhero to overcome them.

The good news is that with each test you overcome, you become stronger. Every time you succeed in making the right choice, you will develop more self-respect and you will act as an inspiration to others. And, with each challenge you overcome, you will make the world that little bit better, and become happier as a result.

Another trick to help increase your happiness and remind yourself why you are taking the hero's journey is to spend regular time in nature. It is, after all, what makes being human possible and what makes a truly sustainable future worth fighting for.

When you are in nature,study it. It is not until we examine nature that we begin to fully appreciate what a miracle it truly is. Contemplate its beauty, its complexity, and its diversity. Also take the time to consider the interconnectedness of your business with all that you see.

When you appreciate how precious nature is, it will help keep you motivated to do something about it,and to stay strong when facing difficult decisions. When we lose touch with nature, it becomes easy to forget the hidden consequences of our life choices and day-to-day decisions.

A SUMMARY OF YOUR SUPERPOWERS

> "We can change the world if we change ourselves. We just
> need to get hold of the old patterns of thinking and
> dealing with things and start listening to our inner voices
> and trusting our own superpowers."
>
> **—Nina Hagen**

As we near the end of our journey together (for now at least), it is time to pause and reflect on your superpowers. Yes, you have them, and we have looked at many already. But in case you missed them . . .

Knowledge

As far back as 1597, Sir Francis Bacon is credited with identifying that knowledge is. You are living in an age with more knowledge available to you via your phone than Bacon had access to his entire life. If knowledge was power in 1597, then in 2017 it is surely a superpower to anyone who chooses to develop and use it.

To make knowledge one of your superpowers create a habit of daily learning and systematic research. Do not blindly accept what you sea and hear, especially when it comes to the news or blogs, as misinformation can severely weaken your powers. Instead take the time to think about what you have learned, and do a little more research if you have any reason to doubt it.

Knowledge helps you find weakness in your enemy, find confidence and strength within yourself, and make more effective decisions. When you build your knowledge about the environment though, it also gives you an invaluable power: motivation. When you learn what is happening in the world, how fragile it truly is, how much damage is taking place and how many lives are being lost under the name of "doing business," you discover real motivation. This motivation can be the driving force behind your mission and will provide you with super stamina.

Ethical Congruency

As you start acting in ways that are congruent with your developing beliefs and understanding, you will find you develop a new level of "presence." People will respond differently to you, and you will find that with each action you take that is congruent with a superhero's ethics, you become stronger and each new decision becomes easier.

This is an almost intangible superpower, but make no mistake, ethical congruency will transform both you and your business. This power can only be developed by acting consistently in ways that align with your core beliefs and values.

When you have ethical congruence, people will begin to trust you more and have faith in your words and your vision. This will become increasingly important as your mission progresses. From your teams and your business partners, to the media and your customers, this trust will prove invaluable.

As Platon Antoniou points out, "The hero is the person who inspires us to think again about our own moral compass, and to think about our own responsibility as global citizens."

Marketing

Sometimes referred to as a form of mind control, marketing is a superpower that has caused incalculable damage when used by unscrupulous people. But like any superpower, it can be used for as much good as it can harm.

As your business grows, so too will its marketing budget and its reach. Though often confused, marketing is more than just advertising or PR. It is a combination of psychology and education that is used to help position your business and presell your prospects. It makes good use of advertising and of sales tools, but it also leverages PR, books, e-mail, partnerships, blogs, live stages, podcasts, and a host of other mediums to achieve its objectives. Sometimes it is very overt, other times extremely covert.

When you learn to master its potential, you have a superpower that can literally move thousands or even millions of people to take action.

(Consider an Apple product launch. You don't think all those people who stood in line waiting for a shop to open did so spontaneously without any direction?)

Charities rely on donations, while government departments rely on limited fixed budgets to fund their messages. Once their budget is spent, they must wait for the next handout. Businesses, on the other hand, are continuously generating revenue, and self-fund the marketing machine. This creates all sorts of exciting possibilities. However, thanks to the potential conflict of interest between the those receiving the message and the business sending it, it also creates an incredible responsibility.

It is the combination of this responsibility and marketing's power that makes it important that we master ethical congruency. Once mastered and in alignment though, we have a real superpower that can not only change the world, but also help save it.

Mind Shield

As we learn to harness and build our superpowers of knowledge, ethical congruence, and marketing, we develop an unintended but useful additional superpower: protection against attacks on our own mind.

These attacks are all around us and are happening on a daily basis. The average person though is all too often unaware and becomes influenced by them. As an RLS you will need to build your defense against such attacks.

These attacks are usually in the form of media, news, other companies' marketing, and current social beliefs and values. Many times these attacks are unintentional, though still potentially harmful to you or your mission. Other times they are deliberately masterminded and take the form of well-orchestrated marketing, or worse, outright propaganda.

As your knowledge grows, you become less accepting of false claims. With ethical congruency, you become more steadfast in your thoughts and your actions. And with mastery of marketing, you begin to recognize the weapons used against you and can more easily deflect their attacks. This mind shield will serve you well and help protect you from being defeated in your quest.

Money

For a long time now big business has used its money to wield power. Corporations have corrupted governments, bribed decision makers, bought and destroyed land, and held contractors for ransom, forcing them to lower costs. Some anarchists and cynics would use this as evidence that money is evil. Of course, it is not money itself that is evil, but those who choose to use its power for self-gain at the cost of others.

Whether we like it or not, money has power, and when in the wrong hands it can do untold damage. The good news is that as your business grows, so will the amount of influence you have through the money that you or your business gets to control.

As an activist, you can chain yourself to a tree and perhaps save a few from being chopped down. As a multimillionaire, you can just buy the lot and protect them without needing much conflict. This is not to discredit the important work of activists in raising awareness, but if you want results, then a lot of money can often go a long way in getting your way. (I just hope by now your way is what is best for everyone!)

In the same way large clothing companies forced manufacturers to reduce costs by threatening to give their business to a competitor, so too are companies like Kathmandu using the same pressure to force manufacturers to look after their staff properly. The power of money can indeed make lives miserable or make them comfortable.

As your business grows so too will your influence on your supply chain, and your responsibility to use that power for good. On a very practical level money is truly a superpower that you will want to master in order to realize your full potential as a Real-Life Superhero.

Your Products

If designed well your products or services can help save the world and will be one of your most tangible superpowers. By providing sustainable solutions to our everyday needs we can reduce the footprint that consumers have while going about their lives. Of course, they also need to be simple, practical, and cost-effective.

Elon Musk is doing this with Tesla, providing cleaner transport, and Solar City, providing cleaner energy. Zenbags is doing this by offering better options for carrying our shopping. Kathmandu and Patagonia are doing this by providing better clothing options. And take for example Ecostore, a company selling household cleaning and personal hygiene products.

If you are developing a new business, look for ways to commercialize new ideas, materials, or scientific breakthroughs that can provide more sustainable alternatives to the current products or services people use. Even if you are providing an accounting, legal, or graphic design service, using the principles in this book will help you provide better alternatives to people's needs and ultimately reduce the negative impact of every one of your customers.

Influence

We have already discussed the power of marketing and money, both of which have their own forms of influence. But as you build all your superpowers, you will develop what is potentially the greatest, yet almost invisible, superpower of all: influence.

We all have influence, just most of us have only a small degree of influence on a small network of people. However, as you grow your business, so too you grow your influence. You affect not only your customers and suppliers, but also your family members, your community, politicians, the media, and other business owners.

It is this last area of influence that makes it a superpower, though it is one that is hard to quantify. A very clear example of this is again Tesla. As I pointed out earlier, Tesla's greatest achievement was not creating an awesome car or a cleaner alternative to current transportation. No, its biggest achievement was in influencing the other car manufacturers to follow suit. The effects of this influence are far more impactful than anything Tesla could have achieved on its own.

By acting as a shining light of inspiration to others, you show them that there can be a better way. Most businesses are so stuck in their old ways or so busy trying to keep things operational that they don't even consider there may be a better way. Leading by example is perhaps one of the most powerful forms of influence, as it puts an end to much debate and demonstrates that an idea can be done.

Just as with all superpowers, influence can be used for good or for evil. Sometimes not being aware of our own powers can have unintended consequences. Children whose parents smoke are between two and four times more likely to also smoke than children whose parents don't smoke. This unintentional influence has cost millions of lives.

On the other hand, celebrities who have understood the power of influence and wanted to do good in the world have leveraged it to get millions of people to take decisive action. The chain reaction and ripple effects of this level of influence are immeasurable. When an individual builds their ability to influence others to the point they can have this type of effect, it truly deserves to be called a real-life superpower.

Some people, like many celebrities, suddenly wake up one day to find they have these powers thrust upon them. They then need to learn how to manage them so as not to do harm. Others understand the potential of influence and spend years deliberately cultivating this superpower. Either way, you should become aware that this is perhaps the master superpower. While you may never get credit for the actions others took as a result of your influence, the results are nonetheless important.

Most of us start out in this world with very little in the way of any superpowers, but we all have the ability to develop them over time. As a business owner, you have more opportunity and more responsibility than most. These powers should not be dismissed or taken lightly. Use them selfishly and you are likely to become the villain of the story. Use them wisely and you will become a Real-Life Superhero.

REAL-LIFE SUPERHERO PROFILE

Business Name: Blue Sphere Media

Business Type: Photography and video production

Founded By: Shawn Heinrichs

Year Established: 2006

Mission: Fuse dramatic imagery with intimate and thought-provoking stories, to connect people to globally important issues and inspire action.

Powers: Create visually and emotionally powerful media addressing critical environmental issues and help save marine species from extinction.

The Story: Like many photographers and videographers, Shawn could have made money working the wedding industry or taking family portraits. Shawn has a greater calling though . . .

In fact, he has no formal training in photography or video. He is entirely self-taught, driven by a desire to use images to expose the devastation that is taking place in our oceans, and to motivate people to do something about it before it's too late.

And so, he developed skills to become an investigative journalist and documentary maker specializing in conservation issues. He has gone undercover to some of the world's toughest and most challenging locations to expose cruelty, illegal trade, and trade creating extinction threats.

He has worked with leading film and journalist teams including CNN's Anderson Cooper and National Geographic to deliver projects for many of the top marine conservation organizations including WildAid, Conservation International, Manta Trust, The Nature Conservancy, and Pew Environment Group.

Shawn's conservation focus includes ending the global slaughter of sharks, protecting manta and mobula rays, and establishing marine protected areas. Indeed, his short movie, Mantas Last Dance, was critical in getting manta rays internationally protected by CITES. Without this project, Manta Rays are likely to have become extinct.

Through his work, he also helped educate fishing communities in Indonesia to stop hunting manta rays, and instead showed them how they can become more profitable by engaging in alternative livelihoods, including sustainable fisheries and eco-tourism.

In 2011 Scuba Diving Magazine gave Shawn the Sea Hero of the Year award, honoring his hard work and the difference he and his company had made.

Talking to Sawn is truly inspirational. His passion and mission are forefront of everything. Despite the technical, logistical, and emotional challenges, the successes make all the hard work rewarding beyond anything else.

It is almost certainly his belief in his mission, unwavering commitment, and sheer determination that inspires others to work with him, and gets him the financial support and exposure he needs to succeed.

His message to everyone though is clear, "If we don't mobilize now, we will lose it all." As he puts it, "we are all drowning, and watching is madness". Waiting until you retire to do something will almost certainly be too late. We need to act now.

Websites: www.bluespheremedia.com

"I THINK THE POWER OF PERSUASION WOULD BE THE GREATEST SUPERPOWER OF ALL TIME." - JENNY MOLLEN

PART 5:
INTO THE FUTURE

"Dreams save us. Dreams lift us up and transform us.
And on my soul I swear... until my dream of a world
where dignity, honor, and justice becomes
the reality we all share... I'll never stop fighting. Ever."

—Superman

FINDING HELP AND SUPPORT

> "I don't want to be around people anymore that judge or talk about what people do. I want to be around people who dream, and support, and do things."
>
> —Amy Poehler

If you read any book or attend any seminar on wealth building, you will hear it repeated again and again: you are the average of the five people you spend the most time with. This is certainly not an exact science, but there is some truth to it.

And it is not just wealth. It applies to political beliefs, level of education, philosophical outlook, morals, etc. So here's the thing: if you want to become a superhero, then you better surround yourself with other heroes.

Find other business owners that are already proving it is possible to live with purpose, make a difference, and generate income at the same time. If you don't already have such a support network, fear not, there are plenty of like-minded people out there. You just need to know where to look.

To help, I have setup an online community for you to get peer support and share contacts, ideas, and other resources. You may also consider joining or starting a group for people in your local area (try meetup. com). The more connections you make and the more support you get, the greater the chances you will succeed in your mission.

Along with the online community group, I also have setup an online resource area with links to the various checklists and worksheets, as well as links to sustainable business directories, information resources, books, documentaries, and other useful sites to help you. There is also a short e-course that will help guide you in taking small daily actions that will compound overtime to make a significant difference.

It is all free, just head over to www.ethicallymad.com/superheroes.

Another way to build a like-minded network is to use your powers of influence to help evolve your existing network. One simple way to do that is to pass this book on and encourage others to read it. If they make even just one or two small changes, it will have helped, and if they decide to embrace the Real-Life Superhero identity fully, then that seemingly insignificant action will have indirectly triggered an avalanche of change.

While we are on the topic of this book, and of influence, if you have found it useful and think the ideas can indeed make a difference, then it would be awesome if you told the world via a review on Amazon or a social media post. (Or perhaps both!)

Good reviews on Amazon make a huge difference in the number of people who see and buy any given book. By leaving a four- or five-star rating, you will help influence others to make the decision to buy, and in doing so be a part of the positive net impact this book has on the world. (And you don't need to have bought the book on Amazon to leave a review.)

By posting on social media sites, more people learn about the book and more people are influenced to buy. Once again, for every person you influence to read the book, you will be a catalyst for all the changes that person makes.

Leaving a review on Amazon and posting to social media take just a couple of minutes. But those couple of minutes could lead to a butterfly effect of change. As Nelson Mandela said, "Action without vision is only passing time, vision without action is merely day dreaming, but vision with action can change the world." Sometimes even the smallest of actions can make a profound difference, even when you don't always see it.

To make it easy for you, I have created a direct link to take you to the Amazon review page: www.ethicallymad.com/x/review

A PREDICTION OF THE FUTURE

> "Nothing we can do can change the past,
> but everything we do changes the future."
> —Ashleigh Brilliant

We live in very uncertain yet exciting times. The future has never been easy to predict, but in many ways, it is now harder than ever before.

If you look at predictions of the present made by futurists of even just twenty years ago, you can see for the most part they were way off the mark. Their projections were based on what they knew, felt, and could imagine then. As Harvard professor Dan Gilbert explains, "We assume what we will feel as we imagine the future is what we'll feel when we get there, but in fact, what we feel as we imagine the future is often a response to what's happening in the present."[167]

Likewise, when we predict the future, it is a reflection of our thoughts, feelings, and knowledge today. Even if we consider something like a utopian future, World War III, or environmental Armageddon, we still can't truly connect to it as being real. We are far too stuck in the reality of our experiences today. But the reality of today will not last long. Change is coming one way or another, and faster than most of us realize.

We are producing pollution at an alarming rate. Many of the world's political leaders remain as corrupt and power-hungry as ever. Big corporations are just getting bigger. Weapons are being developed that can take out small- to medium-sized countries in a single hit. And the weather is becoming increasingly ferocious and damaging.

Yet at the same time, emerging technologies offer to solve more of our problems than ever before. We are now figuring out how to create cleaner energy, manage our land better, gain a deeper understanding of our ecosystems, and produce more sustainable materials, while the Internet continues to decentralize information and create a greater potential for equality.

Technologies such as 3D printing, artificial intelligence, nano-technology, and self-driving vehicles promise to rip apart the very fabric of the way we have done business for centuries. If you think the Internet disrupted many retail and service industries, then hold on tight. I believe that this is nothing compared to what is about to come.

Once 3D printing has been mastered (we are still playing with the relative basics at the moment, but it is evolving quickly), then we will be able to print anything from household goods and electronics to entire cars and houses. This is not going to happen in the next couple of years, but it is going to happen sooner rather than later.

When it does, millions of jobs will be wiped out overnight. On the positive side, with the job losses, we will also stop wasting insane amounts of energy and raw materials. For now, we rely on transporting raw materials to be processed into component parts; these are then shipped around the world to create products, which are then stored in factories and then transported to wholesalers, who ship them to local distributors, who send them to retailers, who then sell them to consumers. Each step of processing, storing, transporting, and selling currently requires many, many people—and a whole lot of energy, pollution, etc.

Advanced 3D printers would allow end consumers to print their products directly using open source plans. The only thing they would require would be the printer (which would be an open source design) and the raw materials (which will become increasingly organic, and many of which will become possible to produce locally).

Sound too far-fetched? Maybe. But consider this: we already have the ability to 3D print plastic, metal, wood, graphene (a semiconductor), recycled concrete, food, and even organic human tissue. Not only that, but we have also already 3D printed household goods, tools, bridges, pizza, body parts, houses, and jet engines.

A quick search online and you will find open source 3D printers and a large number of free 3D print designs for useful tools and household goods. It has yet to become mainstream and has a way to go before it does, but few people realize how much of this prediction already exists.

What about self-driving transport?

A significant percentage of the world's population drive for a living. Trucks, busses, taxis, chauffeurs, couriers, etc. Little do most realize that self-driving technology is all but here. Europe has already begun trialing self-driving trucks and buses, and Uber has started trialing technology for self-driving taxis, while in New Zealand, Domino's Pizza has already delivered pizzas by drone. While not in immediate danger this year, many driving jobs will almost certainly decrease rapidly over the next 10–15 years as self-driving technologies become standardized.

And then there's artificial intelligence...

Once thought of as science fiction, it is now being taken very seriously by the world's greatest minds and has come on in leaps and bounds in just the past few years. Even the likes of Stephen Hawking list it as one of the biggest threats to human existence.

Regardless of whether artificial intelligence does pose a serious threat to humanity or not, it certainly constitutes a threat to more jobs than it creates. Companies are developing artificial intelligence that can fill the roles of humans better than humans can—and this includes legal and medical professionals.

So what does this all mean?

The truth is, it is anyone's guess. Some argue we are moving to economic and social collapse, others toward utopia. One thing is for sure: life will not be the same in the next twenty years. Our technologies, societies and our very realities are radically changing at an exponential rate.

Many people I have spoken to believe our problems would be solved by returning to a simpler life, one of small self-sufficient communities. And this may be true, if it were even remotely likely. Even these idealists usually own cell phones, use transport, and live in the modern world. To locally produce even a fraction of what they are accustomed to using on a daily basis would be not only impractical, but also exceptionally inefficient and costly.

Our future cannot lie in returning to our past. It never has, and never will. Moving forward has always been our only option, whether we like it or not. There is a difference between remembering the wisdom of the past and trying to live in the past. All cultures have evolved over time. Sometimes for the better, sometimes for the worse. Our job is to learn from our mistakes,and craft the future using what we have learned.

Change is a powerful force, and as with any powerful force, resistance only causes stress. When the pressure becomes too much, something must give way, and usually with damaging consequences. Better then to learn from the tai chi master who prefers to predict and redirect force rather than be surprised by its sudden impact or try to stop it once in motion.

As a Real-Life Superhero, your mission to help support and guide humanity through these turbulent times is more important than ever. We need people like you to help find solutions, stay focused on creating positive change, and help spread the message. Together we do create the future.

EPILOGUE

> "It's not who I am underneath,
> but what I do that defines me."
>
> —Batman

Writing this book has had to be the hardest and most emotionally challenging of all the books I have written to date. I have spent countless hours focused on some of humanity's darkest challenges. At times it has made me depressed, other times frustrated and angry, and on occasions physically sick.

I have also been encouraged by the many breakthroughs I have discovered, inspired by the solutions scientists and socialpreneurs are creating every day, and excited by the potential for the future.

It has made me face myself and look at the decisions I have made throughout my life. And it has forced me to examine what I do on a daily basis, both professionally and personally.

And perhaps the most painful realization (and the darkest irony of all) is this: anything that kills people early is currently helping save us as a species. War, disease, famine, natural disasters,etc., all help limit population growth. The larger our population, the greater the demand on limited resources and the greater our pollution levels will be.

Taking the world's population out of poverty seems like a noble course, yet to do so now with the way we currently produce the bulk of our food, products and services, would be a disaster. As horrible as this is to say, our current systems are not sustainable enough for the bottom 80 percent to live like the top 20 percent. Many estimates suggest that we would need between four and five planet earths for every single person in the world to live like the average American.

This may be uncomfortable to accept, but it is the unfortunate situation in which we find ourselves. No hiding from the data will change the facts. We absolutely need to work toward eliminating poverty for all, but we need to ensure that as people are lifted from poverty, we have the solutions in place for long-term sustainability. Unless we do, decent living standards for all will be nothing more than a dream, and war is inevitable as people fight over increasingly limited and insufficient resources.

The path to becoming a superhero requires that we face the dark side, both internally and externally, even though this can be difficult and painful. When dealing with the pain that this can cause, I suggest taking inspiration from the words of Hit Girl . . . " I know it hurts, but maybe that's the real meaning of being a superhero. It is taking that pain and turning it into something good. Something right."

The question remains: are you a part of the solution, or a part of the problem? Being neutral is simply not possible. Sure, you may not be able to fix the world's problems single handedly. And I get it, making small changes can feel insignificant and pointless. But as Vincent van Gogh observed, "Great things are not done by impulse, but by a series of small things brought together."

Each of us maybe small, but we do count, and the little changes do matter. Climate change, environmental pollution, and the current accelerated extinction rates that are taking place are all man made and are serious problems. It is not the end of the world, but it may be the end of man if we don't do something about it now.

It is okay that what we have been doing was wrong. But don't be like the kid who refuses to admit to his mistakes. Man up, admit it, learn from it, and move on. Intelligence is not the ability to avoid mistakes; it is simply capacity to learn from those mistakes and avoid making them again.

A question to ask yourself(without judgment) is, "What was the net social and environmental impact of my life over the past week? The past month? The past year? My life to date?" Is the answer what you would want it to be? If not, why not? What are you going to do about it? And when?

If you have heard me talk or read any of my books before, you will know I am very fond of the phrase, "Life is on average only 4,000 weeks long." Given how many weeks you have already used up and how quickly the past week went, there really is no time like the present to make change!

Writing this book certainly changed my life. I hope that reading it has helped change yours.

As we grow up, for many of us, our parents are our superheroes. I ask you now to join us and become a Real-Life Superhero for your children, grandchildren, and the rest of the world. It is not what you think of yourself, but what you choose to do, or choose not to do, that defines you. H. Jackson Brown Jr. recommended we "Live so that when your children think of fairness, caring and integrity, they think of you." And as Gandhi so eloquently said, "You must be the change you want to see in the world."

Your planet needs you. Not tomorrow. Today . . .

JOIN THE REAL-LIFE SUPERHEROES CLUB (FREE)

SUPPORT, RESOURCES,AND COMMUNITY
www.ethicallymad.com/superheroes

As a reader of this book, you are invited to join the Real-Life Superheroes community and club. There is no cost to become a member, and you will receive a host of benefits that could not be included in this book.

They include:

- A 7-part ethical marketing e-course to help you market and grow your businesses

- A community forum providing support and encouragement from like-minded entrepreneurs and business owners

- Links to various groups, organizations, and directories to help you network with other socially orientated businesses

- Worksheets, videos, and other useful resources to assist you in your training and along your journey

- Links to a variety of useful tools

- Links to socially and environmentally conscious business mentors

- Recommended reading and viewing section

To create your free account, head over to: www.ethicallymad.com/superheroes

ABOUT THE AUTHOR

"it's better to live your own life imperfectly, than to live an imitation of somebody else's life with perfection."

—Bhagavad Gita

Leon Jay is author of four other books on the topics of business and marketing, all of which consistently receive 4 and 5 star reviews. He has spoken on stages around the world, and helped many people grow their businesses, as well as starting many of his own.

After years of teaching business (and mastering imperfection), he realized that too many business owners put an emphasis on making money as their primary purpose for doing business. While money is important, he saw the unintended consequences that this approach was having, and so turned his attention to helping business owners make their businesses become a positive force in society, while still generating the money they needed.

He is now a featured speaker on various stages and podcasts, sharing his passion and insights that have helped business owners see their business in new ways, and find they can get more out of life by focusing on the right priorities in the right order.

If you would like Leon to help your business with sustainability or marketing, visit www.EthicallyMAD.com. Or, to have Leon speak at an event, visit www.leonjay.info.

FOOTNOTES

[1] "Capitalism." Oxford Living Dictionaries. Accessed March 27, 2017. https://en.oxforddictionaries.com/definition/capitalism

[2] Aldous Huxley, Complete Essays 2, 1926-29.

[3] "Poor Air Quality Kills 5.5 Million Worldwide Annually," The University of British Columbia, 2016, accessed March 26, 2017. http://news.ubc.ca/2016/02/12/poor-air-quality-kills-5-5-million-worldwide-annually/

[4] Boris Worm et al, "Impacts of Biodiversity Loss on Ocean Ecosystem Services," Science, 2006, 787-790, accessed March 26, 2017. http://science.sciencemag.org/content/314/5800/787

[5] "An Estimated 12.6 Million Deaths Each Year Are Attributable to Unhealthy Environments," World Health Organization, 2016, accessed March 26, 2017. http://www.who.int/mediacentre/news/releases/2016/deaths-attributable-to-unhealthy-environments/en/

[6] M. Hoffman et al, "The Impact of Conservation on the Status of the World's Vertebrates," Science, 2010, accevssed March 26, 2017.

[7] Fergus Simpson, "Apocalypse Now? Reviving the Doomsday Argument," 2016, accessed March 26, 2017. https://arxiv.org/pdf/1611.03072v1.pdf

[8] "Maternal and Child Nutrition," The Lancet, 2013, accessed March 26, 2017. http://www.thelancet.com/series/maternal-and-child-nutrition

[9] Al Bartlett, Arithmetic, Population and Energy: Sustainability 101, accessed March 26, 2017. http://www.albartlett.org/presentations/arithmetic_population_energy_video1.html

[10] Climate of Concern, 1991, accessed March 26, 2017. https://www.youtube.com/watch?v=cNmuGEBhu38

[11] "Child Mortality Drops by a Third Since 1990," UNICEF, 2010, accessed March, 26, 2017. https://www.unicef.org/media/media_56045.html

[12] "World Development Indicators 2008," World Bank Group, 2008, accessed March 26, 2017. https://openknowledge.worldbank.org/handle/10986/11855

[13] "World's Richest 10% Produce Half of Global Carbon Emissions, Says Oxfam," The Guardian, 2015, accessed March 26, 2017. https://www.theguardian.com/environment/2015/dec/02/worlds-richest-10-produce-half-of-global-carbon-emissions-says-oxfam

[14] Emily Elert, "Daily Infographic: If Everyone Lived Like An American, How Many Earths Would We Need?" Popular Science, 2012, accessed March 26, 2017. http://www.popsci.com/environment/article/2012-10/daily-infographic-if-everyone-lived-american-how-many-earths-would-we-need

[15] "How Many Trees Are Cut Down Each Year?" Reference.com, accessed March 26, 2017. https://www.reference.com/science/many-trees-cut-down-year-2ccceba83de23fdc

[16] "The Extinction Crisis," Center for Biological Diversity, accessed March 26, 2017. http://www.biologicaldiversity.org/programs/biodiversity/elements_of_biodiversity/extinction_crisis/

[17] "Poor Air Quality Kills 5.5 Million Worldwide," The University of British Columbia, 2016, accessed March 26, 2017. http://news.ubc.ca/2016/02/12/poor-air-quality-kills-5-5-million-worldwide-annually/

[18] Susan S. Lang, "Water, Air and Soil Pollution Causes 40 Percent of Deaths Worldwide, Cornell Research Survey Finds," Cornell Chronicle, 2007, accessed March 26, 2017. http://news.cornell.edu/stories/2007/08/pollution-causes-40-percent-deaths-worldwide-study-finds

[19] Susan Goldenberg, "Natural Disasters Displaced More People Than War in 2013, Study Finds," The Guardian, 2014, accessed March 26, 2017. https://www.theguardian.com/world/2014/sep/17/natural-disasters-refugee-people-war-2013-study

[20] Coral Davenport, "Miami Finds Itself Ankle-Deep in Climate Change Debate," The New York Times, 2014, accessed March 26, 2017. https://www.nytimes.com/2014/05/08/us/florida-finds-itself-in-the-eye-of-the-storm-on-climate-change.html?_r=0

[21] Rebecca Kessler, "Fast-Warming Gulf of Maine Offers Hint of Future for Oceans," Yale Environment 360, 2014, accessed March 26, 2017. http://e360.yale.edu/features/fast-warming_gulf_of_maineoffers_hint_of_future_for_oceans

[22] Jeff Masters, "February 2017: Earth's 2nd Warmest February and 4th Warmest Month in Recorded History," Climate Signals Beta, 2017, accessed March 26, 2017. http://www.climatesignals.org/headlines/february-2017-earths-2nd-warmest-february-and-4th-warmest-month-recorded-history

[23] Living Blue Planet Report, WWF, 2015, accessed March 26, 2017. http://assets.worldwildlife.org/publications/817/files/original/Living_Blue_Planet_Report_2015_Final_LR.pdf

[24] "How Much Do We Waste Daily?" Duke University, accessed March, 26, 2017. https://center.sustainability.duke.edu/resources/green-facts-consumers/how-much-do-we-waste-daily

[25] "Major Depression Facts," Clinical-Depression.co.uk, accessed March 26,2017. http://www.clinical-depression.co.uk/dlp/depression-information/major-depression-facts/

[26] Sarah Boseley, "Worldwide Cancer Cases Expected to Soar by 70% Over Next 20 Years," The Guardian, 2014, accessed March 26, 2017. https://www.theguardian.com/society/2014/feb/03/worldwide-cancer-cases-soar-next-20-years

[27] Korin Miller, "Heart Failure Rates Are Rapidly Increasing in the U.S.," Self, 2017, accessed March 26, 2017. http://www.self.com/story/heart-failure-rates-united-states-increasing

[28] David C. Klonoff, "The Increasing Incidence of Diabetes in the 21st Century," J Diabetes Sci Technol, 2009 Jan, 1–2, accessed March 26, 2017. https://www.ncbi.nlm.nih.gov/pmc/articles/PMC2769839/

[29] "Oil," International Energy Agency, accessed March 26, 2017. https://www.iea.org/about/faqs/oil/

[30] T. W. Crowther et al,"Mapping Tree Density at a Global Scale,"Nature, 2015, accessed March 26, 2017. http://www.nature.com/nature/journal/v525/n7568/full/nature14967.html

[31] Arthur Grube et al, Pesticide Industry Sales and Usage: 2006 and 2007 Market Estimates, EPA.gov., 2011, accessed March 26, 2017. https://www.epa.gov/sites/production/files/2015-10/documents/market_estimates2007.pdf

[32] "Plastic Bag Consumption Facts," Conserving Now, accessed March 26, 2017. https://conservingnow.com/plastic-bag-consumption-facts/

[33] "Water Quality," United Nations, accessed March 26, 2017. http://www.un.org/waterforlifedecade/quality.shtml

[34] Matthew Carr and Catherine Airlie, "Global Carbon Emissions Rose by Record Rate Last Year," Bloomberg, 2011, accessed March 26, 2017. http://www.globalcarbonproject.org/carbonbudget/archive/2011/MediaClips_CB2010_3.pdf

[35] David Pimentel and Mario Giampietro, Food, Land, Population and the U.S. Economy, (Carrying Capacity Network, 1994).

[36] Elert, "Daily Infographic: If Everyone Lived Like An American, How Many Earths Would We Need?". http://www.popsci.com/environment/article/2012-10/daily-infographic-if-everyone-lived-american-how-many-earths-would-we-need

[37] Racing Extinction, directed by Louie Psihoyos, 2015. http://racingextinction.com/

[38] The Green Hornet, dir. Michel Gondry, perf. Seth Rogen and Jay Chou (2011), film.

[39] Kris De Decker, "The Monster Footprint of Digital Technology," Low-Tech Magazine, 2009. http://www.lowtechmagazine.com/2009/06/embodied-energy-of-digital-technology.html

[40] "Sustainable Development," Wikipedia, accessed March 26, 2017. https://en.wikipedia.org/wiki/Sustainable_development

[41] "Embodied Energy" Wikipedia, accessed March 26, 2017. https://en.wikipedia.org/wiki/Embodied_energy

[42] David Thomas, "The Carbon Credentials of Smartphones," Ecologist, accessed March 26, 2017. http://www.theecologist.org/green_green_living/2084407/the_carbon_credentials_of_smartphones.html

[43] "27-Inch iMac with Retina 5K Display Environmental Report," Apple, 2015, accessed March 26, 2017. http://images.apple.com/environment/pdf/products/desktops/27inch_iMacR5K_PER_Oct2015.pdf

[44] "The Carbon Footprint of Everyday Objects," Sustainability for All, accessed March 26, 2017. http://www.activesustainability.com/the-carbon-footprint-of-everyday-objects

[45] Our Common Future, World Commission on Environment and Development, 1987, 16, accessed March 26, 2017. http://www.un-documents.net/our-common-future.pdf

[46] J. B. MacKinnon, "The LED Quandary: Why There's No Such Thing as "Built to Last," The New Yorker, 2016, accessed March 26, 2017. http://www.newyorker.com/business/currency/the-l-e-d-quandary-why-theres-no-such-thing-as-built-to-last

[47] Signe Dean, "A Chemical Plant in India Is Producing Baking Soda from Co2 Emissions,"National Geographic, 2017, accessed March 26, 2017. http://www.nationalgeographic.com.au/science/a-chemical-plant-in-india-is-producing-baking-soda-from-co2-emissions.aspx

[48] Spiderman 2, directed by Sam Raimi, performed by Tobey Maguire and Kirsten Dunst, US (Sony, 2002).

[49] "Industrial Air Pollution Has High Economic Cost," European Environment Agency, 2016, accessed March 26, 2017. http://www.eea.europa.eu/media/newsreleases/industrial-air-pollution-has-high

[50] "Leonardo DiCaprio: Climate Fight Is US History's 'Biggest Economic Opportunity,'"The Guardian, 2016, accessed March 26, 2017. https://www.theguardian.com/environment/2016/dec/17/leonardo-dicaprio-climate-change-united-nations

[51] Puja Modal, "Air Pollution: Essay on the Effects of Air Pollution on Human, Animals and Plants (with Statistics)," Your Article Library, accessed March 20, 2017. http://www.yourarticlelibrary.com/essay/air-pollution-essay-on-the-effects-of-air-pollution-on-human-animals-and-plants-with-statistics/28316/

[52] "How Much Do Oceans Add to World's Oxygen?" Earth & Sky, 2015. http://earthsky.org/earth/how-much-do-oceans-add-to-worlds-oxygen

[53] "Oceans and the Carbon Cycle," The Global Development Research Center, accessed March 26, 2017. https://www.gdrc.org/oceans/fsheet-02.html

[54] Algalita Marine Research Foundation Annual Report 2008, Algalita.org, 2008, accessed March 26, 2017. http://www.algalita.org/wp-content/uploads/2014/06/2008AnnualReport.pdf

[55] "Plastic Statistics," Ocean Crusaders, accessed March 26, 2017. http://oceancrusaders.org/plastic-crusades/plastic-statistics/

[56] "Where Is Earth's Water?", The USGS Science School, accessed March 26, 2017. https://water.usgs.gov/edu/earthwherewater.html

[57] "Irrigation Water Use," The USGS Science School, accessed March 26, 2017. https://water.usgs.gov/edu/wuir.html

[58] "Plastic Statistics," Ocean Crusaders. http://oceancrusaders.org/plastic-crusades/plastic-statistics/

[59] Jenna R. Jambeck et al, "Plastic Waste Inputs from Land into the Ocean," Science, 2015 768-771, accessed March 26, 2017. http://science.sciencemag.org/content/347/6223/768.full

[60] "Kiwanis International Six Cents Initiative," UNICEF USA, accessed March 26, 2017. https://www.unicefusa.org/supporters/organizations/

civil-society/partners/kiwanis/circle-k/six-cents-initiative

61 Algalita Marine Research Foundation Annual Report 2008, Algalita. org, 2008, accessed March 26, 2017. http://www.algalita.org/wp-content/uploads/2014/06/2008AnnualReport.pdf

62 "Nonpoint Pointers: Nonpoint Source Pollution: The Nation's Largest Water Quality Problem, Pointer No. 1," EPA.gov, 1996, accessed March 26, 2017. https://goo.gl/KpFJKb

63 "A Single Drop of Motor Oil Can Contaminate a Million Drops of Water," Used Oil Recycling, accessed March 26, 2017. http://usedoilrecycling. com/resources/file/BC/Ambassador Brochure_Web.pdf

64 http://grantham.sheffield.ac.uk/how-to-reduce-the-environmental-impact-of-a-loaf-of-bread/, University of Sheffield, accessed April 14, 2017

65 "Secretary-General's message on the International Day for Biological Diversity," United Nations, 2012, accessed March 26, 2017. https:// www.un.org/sg/en/content/sg/statement/2012-05-22/secretary-generals-message-international-day-biological-diversity

66 Ransom A. Myers and Boris Worm, "Rapid Worldwide Depletion of Predatory Fish Communities," Nature, v.423, May 2013.

67 "Hunger Stats," World Food Programme, accessed March 26, 2017. http://www1.wfp.org/zero-hunger

68 "Food: Too Good to Waste Implementation Guide and Toolkit," EPA, 2016, accessed March 26, 2017. https://www.epa.gov/sites/production/files/2016-02/documents/implementation_guide_and_toolkit_ftgtw_2_1_2016_pubnumberadded508_alldocuments.pdf

69 "How much water goes into producing our food and drink? - in pictures," The Guardian, 2013, accessed March 26, 2017. https://www. theguardian.com/sustainable-business/gallery/how-much-water-to-make-food-drink

70 Brian Vinh Tien Trinh,"Earth Day 2012: The Most Harmful Foods For The Environment," The Huffington Post Canada, 2012, accessed March

26, 2017. http://www.huffingtonpost.ca/2012/04/05/earth-day-2012-the-most-harmful-foods_n_1402771.html

[71] Rhitu Chatterjee,"What's the Environmental Footprint of a Loaf of Bread?", NPR, 2017, accessed March 26, 2017. http://www.npr.org/sections/thesalt/2017/02/27/517531611/whats-the-environmental-footprint-of-a-loaf-of-bread-now-we-know

[72] "The 59 Ingredients in a Fast-Food Strawberry Milkshake," The Guardian, 2006, accessed March 26, 2017. https://www.theguardian.com/news/2006/apr/24/food.foodanddrink

[73] "Recent Trends in GE Adoption," USDA, 2016, accessed March 26, 2017. https://www.ers.usda.gov/data-products/adoption-of-genetically-engineered-crops-in-the-us/recent-trends-in-ge-adoption.aspx

[74] Jaime Dolmage, "Shut the Front Door! If We Ate Less Meat, This Is What Would Happen to the Planet," One Green Planet, 2016, accessed March 26, 2017. http://www.onegreenplanet.org/animalsandnature/eat-for-the-planet-meat-and-the-environment/acc

[75] Fergus Simpson, "Apocalypse Now? Reviving the Doomsday Argument," 2016, accessed March 26, 2017. https://arxiv.org/pdf/1611.03072v1.pdf

[76] "Energy Access Database," World Energy Outlook, accessed March 26, 2017. http://www.worldenergyoutlook.org/resources/energydevelopment/energyaccessdatabase/

[77] "Global Greenhouse Emissions Data," EPA, accessed March 26, 2017. https://www.epa.gov/ghgemissions/global-greenhouse-gas-emissions-data

[78] "Statistics," International Energy Agency, accessed March 26, 2017. https://www.iea.org/statistics/statisticssearch/report/?year=2014&country=USA&product=Indicators

[79] "Statistics," International Energy Agency, accessed March 26, 2017. https://www.iea.org/statistics/statisticssearch/report/?year=2014&country=CHINA&product=RenewablesandWaste

[80] "International Energy Statistics," US Department of Energy, EIA, accessed March 26, 2017. https://www.eia.gov/beta/international/data/browser/#/?vs=INTL.44-1-AFRC-QBTU.A&vo=0&v=H&start=1980&end=2014

[81] Matt McGrath, "World's Poorest Countries to Aim for 100% Green Energy," BBC, 2016, accessed March 26, 2017. http://www.bbc.com/news/science-environment-38028130

[82] Tim Buckley, "India cancels four major new coal plants in move to end imports," Renew Economy, 2016, accessed March 26, 2017. http://reneweconomy.com.au/india-cancels-four-major-new-coal-plants-in-move-to-end-imports-27494/

[83] Mike Burners Lee and Duncan Clark, "What's the Carbon Footprint of ... Email?" The Guardian, 2010, accessed March 26, 2017. https://www.theguardian.com/environment/green-living-blog/2010/oct/21/carbon-footprint-email

[84] "Cool Biz Campaign," Wikipedia, accessed March 26, 2017. https://en.wikipedia.org/wiki/Cool_Biz_campaign

[85] "Cleaner Power Plants," EPA, accessed March 26, 2017. https://www.epa.gov/mats/cleaner-power-plants

[86] Toxic Power: How Power Plants Contaminate Our Air and States, NRDC, 2011, accessed March 26, 2017. https://www.nrdc.org/sites/default/files/air_11072001a.pdf

[87] Paul Lester, "4 Ways to Slay Energy Vampires this Halloween," Energy.gov., 2015, accessed March 26, 2017. http://standby.lbl.gov/faq.html

[88] "Frequently Asked Questions," Standby Power, accessed March 26, 2017. http://standby.lbl.gov/faq.html

[89] "World Coal Consumption by Year," Index Mundi, accessed March 26, 2017. http://www.indexmundi.com/energy/?product=coal&graph=consumption

[90] "Lighting Choices to Save You Money," Energy.gov, accessed March 26, 2017. https://energy.gov/energysaver/lighting-choices-save-you-money

91 "Statistics," International Energy Agency, accessed March 26, 2017. https://www.iea.org/statistics/statisticssearch/report/?year=2014&country=USA&product=Indicators

92 "Energy Access Database," International Energy Agency, accessed March 26, 2017. http://www.worldenergyoutlook.org/resources/energydevelopment/energyaccessdatabase/

93 "Globetrotting Food Will Travel Farther Than Ever This Thanksgiving," Worldwatch Institute, accessed March 26, 2017. http://www.worldwatch.org/globetrotting-food-will-travel-farther-ever-thanksgiving

94 "Carbon Emissions," World Shipping Council, accessed March 26, 2017. http://www.worldshipping.org/industry-issues/environment/air-emissions/carbon-emissions

95 "Environmental Impact of Shipping," Wikipedia, accessed March 26, 2017. https://en.wikipedia.org/wiki/Environmental_impact_of_shipping#cite_note-Schrooten1-22

96 Arthur J. Miller, Yardbird Blues, "Part 20 - Greed Upon the Oceans: Flag of Convenience Ships," Industrial Workers of the World, accessed March 26, 2017. http://www.iww.org/unions/iu510/yardbird/yardbird20.shtml

97 https://www.transportenvironment.org/press/50000-heart-deaths-year-caused-traffic-noise, Transport and Environment, accessed April 14, 2017

98 Duncan Clark, "Business Class Fliers Leave Far Larger Carbon Footprint," The Guardian, 2010, accessed March 26, 2017. https://www.theguardian.com/environment/blog/2010/feb/17/business-class-carbon-footprint

99 Brian McKensie and Melanie Rapino, "Commuting in the United States: 2009," Census.gov, 2011, accessed March 26, 2017. https://www.census.gov/prod/2011pubs/acs-15.pdf

100 Duncan Clark, "Business Class Fliers Leave Far Larger Carbon Footprint," The Guardian, 2010, accessed March 26, 2017. https://

www.theguardian.com/environment/blog/2010/feb/17/business-class-carbon-footprint

[101] Holly Heinrich, "Why It's Cheaper to Charge an Electric Car than Fill Up with Gas," State Impact, 2013 accessed March 26, 2017. https://stateimpact.npr.org/texas/2013/06/12/why-its-cheaper-to-charge-an-electric-car-than-fill-up-with-gas/

[102] Al Yates, "Pump Vs Plug: Cradle to Grave Impacts of Electric Vehicles," Ecotricity, 2016, accessed March 26, 2017.

[103] "Average Annual Miles per Driver by Age Group," Federal Highway Administration, 2016, accessed March 26, 2017. https://www.fhwa.dot.gov/ohim/onh00/bar8.htm

[104] "Reducing Emissions from Transport,"European Commission, accessed March 26, 2017. https://ec.europa.eu/clima/policies/transport_en

[105] "Globetrotting Food Will Travel Farther Than Ever This Thanksgiving," Worldwatch Institute, accessed March 26, 2017. http://www.worldwatch.org/globetrotting-food-will-travel-farther-ever-thanksgiving

[106] Fred Pearce, "How 16 Ships Create as Much Pollution as All the Cars in the World," Daily Mail, 2009, accessed March 26, 2017. http://www.dailymail.co.uk/sciencetech/article-1229857/How-16-ships-create-pollution-cars-world.html

[107] Ibrahim Dincer and Calin Zamfirescu, Sustainable Energy Systems and Applications, (Springer 2011), 84, accessed March 26, 2017. https://books.google.co.nz/

[108] Plastics the Facts 2014/2015, Plastics Europe, accessed March 26, 2017. http://www.plasticseurope.org/documents/document/20150227150049-final_plastics_the_facts_2014_2015_260215.pdf

[109] Nicole D'Alessandro, "22 Facts About Plastic Pollution (And 10 Things We Can Do About It)," EcoWatch, 2014, accessed March 26, 2017.

http://www.ecowatch.com/22-facts-about-plastic-pollution-and-10-things-we-can-do-about-it-1881885971.html

[110] "Plastic 'Nurdles' Found Littering UK Beaches," BBC, 2017, accessed March 26, 2017. http://www.bbc.com/news/uk-39001011

[111] The New Plastics Economy: Rethinking the Future of Plastics, Ellen MacArthur Foundation, 2016, accessed March 26, 2017. https://www.ellenmacarthurfoundation.org/assets/downloads/news/New-Plastics-Economy_Background-to-Key-Statistics_19022016v2.pdf

[112] Plastics of Europe, "World Plastics Production 1950 – 2015," Committee.iso.org, accessed March 26, 2017. https://committee.iso.org/files/live/sites/tc61/files/The Plastic Industry Berlin Aug 2016 - Copy.pdf

[113] Tracking Trash: 25 Years of Action for the Ocean, Ocean Conservancy, 2011, accessed March 26, 2017. http://act.oceanconservancy.org/pdf/Marine_Debris_2011_Report_OC.pdf

[114] Richard Grey, "Plankton Are Eating PLASTIC: Feasting on Ocean Litter Could Devastate Marine Ecosystems, Scientists Warn," Daily Mail, 2015, accessed March 26, 2017. http://www.dailymail.co.uk/sciencetech/article-3152368/Plankton-eating-PLASTIC-Feasting-ocean-litter-devastate-marine-ecosystems-scientists-warn.html

[115] Jenna R. Janbeck et al, "Plastic Waste Inputs from Land into the Ocean," Science, 2015, 768-771, accessed March 26, 2017. http://science.sciencemag.org/content/347/6223/768

[116] Kari O'Conner, "How Long Does It Take a Plastic Bottle to Biodegrade?" Postconsumers.com, 2011, accessed March 26, 2017. http://www.postconsumers.com/education/how-long-does-it-take-a-plastic-bottle-to-biodegrade/

[117] Charles Fishman, "Message in a Bottle," Fast Company Magazine, 2007, accessed March 26, 2017. https://www.fastcompany.com/59971/message-bottle

[118] "Statistics," International Energy Agency.

[119] Sarah Kaplan, "By 2050, there Will Be More Plastic than Fish in the

World's Oceans, Study Says," Washington Post, 2016, accessed March 26, 2017. https://www.washingtonpost.com/news/morning-mix/wp/2016/01/20/by-2050-there-will-be-more-plastic-than-fish-in-the-worlds-oceans-study-says/?utm_term=.b2f6c2d04220

[120] "Issues," Time for Change, accessed March 26, 2017. http://www.timeforchange.org/are-cows-cause-of-global-warming-meat-methane-CO2

[121] Drew T. Shindell et al, "Improved Attribution of Climate Forcing to Emissions,"Science, 2009, 716-718, accessed March 26, 2017. http://science.sciencemag.org/content/326/5953/716.figures-only

[122] Farm Safety Association, "Manure Gas Dangers," National Ag Safety Database, 2002, accessed March 26, 2017. http://nasdonline.org/48/d001616/manure-gas-dangers.html

[123] "Livestock a Major Threat to Environment," FAO Newsroom, 2006, accessed March 26, 2017. http://www.fao.org/Newsroom/en/news/2006/1000448/index.html

[124] Wageningen University and Research Centre, "Agriculture is the Direct Driver for Worldwide Deforestation," Science Daily, 2012, accessed March 26, 2017. https://www.sciencedaily.com/releases/2012/09/120925091608.htm

[125] "Forests," GreenFacts, accessed March 26, 2017. http://www.greenfacts.org/en/forests/index.htm#2

[126] David Pimental et al, "Water Resources: Agricultural and Environmental Issues." BioScience,2004, 909-18, accessed March 26, 2017. https://academic.oup.com/bioscience/article/54/10/909/230205/Water-Resources-Agricultural-and-Environmental

[127] Nancy L. Barber, "Summary of estimated water use in the United States in 2005," USGS, 2009, accessed March 26, 2017. https://pubs.usgs.gov/fs/2009/3098/

[128] "Protein," Harvard T.H. Chan, accessed March 26, 2017. https://www.hsph.harvard.edu/nutritionsource/what-should-you-eat/protein/

[129] Sabine Rohrmann et al, "Meat consumption and mortality - results from the European Prospective Investigation into Cancer and Nutrition," BMC Medicine, accessed March 26, 2017. http://bmcmedicine. biomedcentral.com/articles/10.1186/1741-7015-11-63

[130] James Cameron, "James Cameron: Halting Climate Change Is as Simple as Changing Our Diets," Newsweek, 2015, accessed March 26, 2017. http://www.newsweek.com/james-cameron-halting-climate-change-simple-change-diets-402447

[131] John P. Reganold and Jonathan M. Wachter, "Organic Agriculture in the Twenty-First Century," Nature, 2016, accessed March 26, 2017. https://goo.gl/L1B4Sr

[132] Marco Springmann et al, "Analysis and Valuation of the Health and Climate Change Cobenefits of Dietary Change," PNAS, 2016, accessed March 26, 2017. http://www.pnas.org/content/113/15/4146.full

[133] International Agency for Research on Cancer, WHO, Monographs evaluate consumption of red meat and processed meat, accessed June 24, 2017. http://www.iarc.fr/en/media-centre/pr/2015/pdfs/pr240_E. pdf

[134] "The Hamburger Footprint – How Much Energy Does It Take?" Source Power and Gas, 2014. http://www.spgenergy.com/blog/the-hamburger-footprint-how-much-energy-does-it-take/

[135] "Facts," Cowspiracy, accessed March 26, 2017. http://www. cowspiracy.com/facts/

[136] Sergio Margulis, "Causes of Deforestation of the Brazilian Amazon," The World Bank, 2004, accessed March 26, 2017. https:// openknowledge.worldbank.org/handle/10986/15060

[137] Damian Carrington, "Amazon Deforestation Increased by One-Third in Past Year," The Guardian, 2013, accessed March 26, 2017. https://www. theguardian.com/environment/2013/nov/15/amazon-deforestation-increased-one-third

[138] "Risk Management Evaluation for Concentrated Animal Feeding Operations," US EPA National Risk Management Laboratory, 2004,

accessed March 26, 2017. https://goo.gl/jifYGM

[139] J. Matthew Roney, "Taking Stock: World Fish Catch Falls to 90 Million Tons in 2012," Earth Policy Institute, 2012, accessed March 26, 2017. http://www.earth-policy.org/indicators/C55/fish_catch_2012

[140] Peter Scarborough et al, "Dietary Greenhouse Gas Emissions of Meat-Eaters, Fish-Eaters, Vegetarians and Vegans in the UK," Climatic Change, 2004, 179-192, accessed March 26, 2017. https://link.springer.com/article/10.1007%2Fs10584-014-1169-1

[141] "Is Meat Sustainable?" Worldwatch Institute, 2004, accessed March 26, 2017. http://www.worldwatch.org/node/549

[142] "Issues," Time for Change. http://www.timeforchange.org/are-cows-cause-of-global-warming-meat-methane-CO2

[143] Kelly Bryant, "You Won't Believe How Much Clothing the US Throws Away in a Year," Takepart, 2015, accessed March 26, 2017. http://www.takepart.com/video/2015/05/29/clothes-trash-landfill

[144] Kelly Bryant, "You Won't Believe How Much Clothing the US Throws Away in a Year," Takepart, 2015, accessed March 26, 2017. http://www.takepart.com/video/2015/05/29/clothes-trash-landfill

[145] "Municipal Solid Waste in the United States: 2009 Facts and Figures," EPA, 2009, accessed March 26, 2017. https://archive.epa.gov/epawaste/nonhaz/municipal/web/pdf/msw2009rpt.pdf

[146] Pamela Ravasio, "How Can We Stop Water from Becoming a Fashion Victim?" The Guardian, 2012, accessed March 26, 2017. https://www.theguardian.com/sustainable-business/water-scarcity-fashion-industry

[147] "The Impact of a Cotton T-Shirt," WWF, 2013, accessed March 26, 2017. https://www.worldwildlife.org/stories/the-impact-of-a-cotton-t-shirt

[148] Environmental Justice Foundation, The Deadly Chemicals in Cotton, EJFoundation.org, 2007, 2, accessed March 26, 2017. http://ejfoundation.org/sites/default/files/public/the_deadly_chemicals_in_cotton.pdf

[149] Melody Meyer, "Chemical Cotton," Rodale Institute, 2014, accessed March 26, 2017. https://rodaleinstitute.org/chemical-cotton/

[150] Bradley Blackburn, "Are Your Clothes 'Made in America'?" ABC News, 2011, accessed March 26, 2017. https://rodaleinstitute.org/chemical-cotton/

[151] Peter Lehner, "An Inside Look at a Cleaner Textile Mill in China," NDRC, 2011, accessed March 26, 2017. https://www.nrdc.org/experts/peter-lehner/inside-look-cleaner-textile-mill-china

[152] Melissa Bryer, "25 Shocking Fashion Industry Statistics," Treehugger, 2012, accessed March 26, 2017. http://www.treehugger.com/sustainable-fashion/25-shocking-fashion-industry-statistics.html

[153] Harry Bradford, "Bangladesh to Raise Minimum Wage for Garment Workers," Huffington Post, 2013, accessed March 26, 2017. http://www.huffingtonpost.com/2013/05/12/bangladesh-minimum-wage-garment-workers_n_3263347.html

[154] Michael Cooney, "Computer Factories Eat Way More Energy than Running the Devices They Build," Network World, 2011, accessed March 26, 2017. http://www.networkworld.com/article/2229029/data-center/computer-factories-eat-way-more-energy-than-running-the-devices-they-build.html

[155] "The Perils of Gold Mining:'A Wedding Ring Produces 20 Tons of Waste'," Spiegel Online, 2008, accessed March 26, 2017. http://www.spiegel.de/international/world/the-perils-of-gold-mining-a-wedding-ring-produces-20-tons-of-waste-a-542561.html

[156] "Industry Release," EPA.gov, 2017, accessed March 26, 2017. https://goo.gl/yxCJOO

[157] "Dirty Metals" Infographic, EarthWorks, 2015, accessed March 26, 2017.

[158] "Environmental Impact," The Greener Diamond, accessed March 26, 2017. http://thegreenerdiamond.org/conflict-diamonds-2/environmental-impact/

[159] "Coal-Mine-Drainage Projects in Pennsylvania," USGS, accessed

March 26, 2017. https://pa.water.usgs.gov/projects/energy/amd/

[160] "Gold Mining and Labor Concerns," Brilliant Earth, accessed March 26, 2017. https://goo.gl/y1l3AZ

[161] EARTHWORKS and MiningWatch Canada, "How Mine Waste Dumping is Poisoning Our Oceans, Rivers, and Lakes," No Dirty Gold, 2012, accessed March 26, 2017. http://nodirtygold.earthworksaction. org/library/detail/troubled_waters#.WNISU_nyvIU

[162] "Chevron's Chernobyl in the Amazon," Amazon Watch, accessed March 26, 2017. http://amazonwatch.org/work/chevron

[163] Jean-Robert Wells et al, "Carbon Footprint Assessment of a Paperback Book - Can Planned Integration of Deinked Market Pulp be Detrimental to Climate?" Research Gate, 2012, accessed March 26, 2017. https:// goo.gl/OvWOBR

[164] "Gartner Says Worldwide Sales of Smartphones Grew 7 Percent in the Fourth Quarter of 2016," Gartner, 2017, accessed March 26, 2017. http://www.gartner.com/newsroom/id/3609817

[165] "What Is Biodiversity?" WWF, accessed March 26, 2017. http://wwf. panda.org/about_our_earth/biodiversity/biodiversity/

[166] Richard Feloni, "Richard Branson shares the first question he asks every entrepreneur who comes to him for advice," Business Insider, 2016, accessed March 26, 2017. http://www.businessinsider.com/ richard-branson-advice-for-entrepreneurs-2016-11

[167] Daniel Gilbert, Stumbling on Happiness, (Alfred A. Knopf, 2006).